MARRIAGE: DISILLUSION AND HOPE

Papers Celebrating
Forty Years
of the
Tavistock Institute
of Marital Studies

MARRIAGE: DISILLUSION AND HOPE

Papers Celebrating
Forty Years
of the Tavistock Institute
of Marital Studies

edited by

Christopher Clulow

published for

The Tavistock Institute
of Marital Studies

London

by

Karnac Books

London   1990   New York

First published in 1990 by
H. Karnac (Books) Ltd.
58 Gloucester Road
London SW7 4QY

Distributed in the United States of America by
Brunner/Mazel, Inc.
19 Union Square West
New York, NY 10003

Copyright © 1990
by The Tavistock Institute of Medical Psychology

All rights reserved. No part of this book may be reproduced,
in any form, by any process or technique,
without the prior written permission of the publisher.

British Library Cataloguing in Publication Data
  Marriage: disillusion and hope
  1. Marriage.
  I. Clulow, Christopher   II. Tavistock Institute of
  Marital Studies
  306.81
  ISBN 0-946439-93-1

Printed in Great Britain by BPCC Wheatons Ltd, Exeter

CONTENTS

Introduction   1

PART ONE
Marriage: public and private agendas

Remarks on an anniversary
  Timothy Renton
    Minister of State, Home Office   7

The Tavistock Institute of Marital Studies in retrospect
  Christopher Clulow
    Chairman, TIMS   13

Marriage and Social Change
  David Clark
    Sociologist, Department of Health Studies,
    Sheffield City Polytechnic   23

Marriage and personal change
  Robin Skynner
    Psychiatrist, Group-Analytic Practice   33

Changing marriage
Barbara Dearnley
Marital Psychotherapist, TIMS   43

Reactions and comments   55

List of guests   61

PART TWO
The Tavistock Institute of Marital Studies: evolution of a marital agency
Douglas Woodhouse
Past Chairman, TIMS

Introduction   71

Historical development   73

Theoretical development   101

References   121

MARRIAGE: DISILLUSION AND HOPE

Papers Celebrating
Forty Years
of the
Tavistock Institute
of Marital Studies

INTRODUCTION

The Tavistock Institute of Marital Studies began life as the Family Discussion Bureau on 20 September 1948. In its forty-year history it has developed into a specialist organisation. It is a centre of advanced study and practice which has grown up within the psychoanalytic tradition and is committed to promoting understanding and good practice among those who work with couples and families. By offering psychotherapy to couples, mounting programmes of training and consultation for practitioners, and undertaking research it has contributed, and continues to contribute, to understanding and alleviating the stresses of family life.

On 8 July 1988, these achievements were marked by an anniversary conference entitled 'Marriage: Disillusion and Hope'. This seemed a fitting way to celebrate a birthday, and the event became what Professor Dunstan, Chairman of the Council of the TIMS' parent body (the Tavistock Institute of Medical Psychology) called, in his opening words of welcome to guests, a 'working party'. In the elegant surroundings of the Royal Society of Medicine in London, two hundred people representing the helping professions, the church, education (including the media), the law and industry met to consider changes which have affected the institution of marriage during the post-war years, and what implications these changes might have for the future.

The Institute has decided to publish the papers given at the conference for two reasons. The first is largely internal and to do with commemorating and recording a significant point reached in the history of the TIMS. The second is because we believe the issues raised in the papers and discussion are highly relevant to the mental health of individuals, families and the community in the closing years of this century. It is a central tenet of psychoanalytic thought that an understanding of history, personal and collective, is the key to building upon rather than repeating the past. However, the process of remembering, let alone understanding, can be extremely difficult when the busy-ness of present-day life shuts out all but what immediately confronts us. Time out to reflect on the past is, then, no indulgence, but a means of building for the future.

So these papers touch not only upon the history of an organisation, but also upon part of the history of the institution of marriage as well as some of the thinking that has gone on over the past forty years about how best to help improve the quality of family life. For TIMS, and perhaps for others working in this field, the papers may provide the springboard for a new period of activity.

Part One of this monograph reproduces the papers as they were given at the conference, including some of the personal asides made by speakers which convey something of the informal and celebratory tone of the meeting. The business of helping troubled marriages is carried out in a political and social context, and the opening papers outline some of the opportunities and constraints defined by the socio-political backdrop of the years 1948 to 1988 in the United Kingdom. Timothy Renton, then Minister of State at the Home Office, offers some personal reflections on marriage and highlights the criteria of partnership, enterprise and relevance in directing government policy towards funding non-government organisations. David Clark, a sociologist and former Director of the Scottish Marriage Guidance Council, identifies three phases in the legal de-regulation of marriage in the post-war years and considers the move away from a preoccupation with marriage as the normative basis for adult relationships. Sandwiched between these papers is a retrospective account of how the Tavistock Institute of Marital Studies has developed against this background.

The next two papers consider how family tensions have been understood in a personal context over the past forty years and describe some ways in which this understanding has been put to use. Robin Skynner outlines how some of the key ways of thinking about relationships have evolved, and he draws attention to changes that have taken place in relationships between men and women. Barbara Dearnley, a marital psychotherapist with TIMS, makes four key points about the potential of therapeutic help to change marriage.

Following these papers I have attempted to bring together three major and interrelated themes which dominated the discussion: relationships between men and women; relationships between work and home; and relationships between those who control resources and those who need them (with particular reference to the public funding of the personal services). Part One concludes with a list of guests who accepted invitations to attend the conference.

Part Two reproduces a detailed and systematic study of the evolution of the Tavistock Institute of Marital Studies as a case study in organisational development. This paper traces not only the development of a non-medical marital agency but also the evolution and application of analytic theory in an organisational context. A shortened version of this paper will appear in E. Trist and H. Murray (editors), *The Social Engagement of Social Science* Volume I, to be published by the University of Pennsylvania Press in June 1990. Douglas Woodhouse was Chairman of TIMS for seventeen years of its forty-year history, and it is very appropriate that this paper should appear in a volume which celebrates the ruby anniversary of the Institute.

Christopher Clulow
Chairman, TIMS

PART ONE

Marriage: public and private agendas

Remarks on an anniversary

Timothy Renton

I have always had a very great nervousness about speaking into microphones ever since my good friend the Bishop of Jarrow told me how he was taking a communion service, I think in one of the new series, in a very large cathedral—it might have been Durham—and, as everyone was ready for the service to start, he noticed that the microphone was not working. So he turned to the curate by his side and said 'there's something wrong with the microphone'. The congregation, seeing his lips move, immediately chanted back 'and also with you'. One of the dangers of Series Two, perhaps.

I am delighted, flattered and honoured to have been invited to open this meeting of the Institute of Marital Studies on this very happy occasion of your fortieth anniversary and to take part in what Professor Gordon Dunstan has described as your 'party'. Many of you will remember the words of the Harrow School song, '40 years on and afar and a sunder parted are those who are singing today'. The list of those attending this meeting gives the lie to that song. Forty years on and you have gathered together a most impressive collection of informed and interesting people. I was reading the list of your participants out of my red box last night and I thought it read like a *Who's Who* of the marriage guidance, the family, the health and the social work world. It says a very great deal for the work and reputation of your Institute that it has attracted such a distinguished audience on this fortieth anniversary.

Professor Dunstan, you said kind words about me, and about the Home Office, but I am here, I have to say, under false pretences. You invited the Home Secretary and he would indeed have wished to come but unfortunately he was already committed to be in another part of the country today. I bring his best wishes and those of my Ministerial colleague, John Patten, who has a direct responsibility for this subject and for your funding at the Home Office. I realise you may feel that you have invited Hamlet and ended up by only getting Banquo. However, I have at least one important credential for being here today, and this is that my wife and I have been happily married for 28 years and we have five children, and for that reason I have some personal experience as what you might call a customer of marital studies.

I have often been struck how quickly one moves, in literature and society, from marriage being praised and serenaded when any couple is in the engagement stage, or on their wedding day or on their honeymoon, how quickly marriage moves from that to being an estate that is so often laughed at and derided, either in novels, the daily press or on the stage or television. The Prayer Book refers to matrimony as 'an honourable estate instituted of God in the time of man's innocency [what a lovely word that is] signifying unto us the mystical union that is betwixt Christ and his Church'. An honourable estate. Yet you would hardly think that if you made a compendium of the wise and witty sayings that have been made about marriage. For example, the remark attributed to Erica Jong the author: 'bigamy is having one husband too many. Monogamy is the same'. Or again, Noel

Coward: 'I have sometimes thought of marrying and then I have thought again'. And then the sad remark by the writer Gerald Brenan: 'marriage is an arrangement by which two people start by getting the best out of each other and often end by getting the worst'.

Let me balance that with a quotation from Andre Maurois: 'a happy marriage is a long conversation which always seems too short'. But the fact of the matter is that for many people marriage, a totally monogamous relationship, lasting twenty, thirty, forty years, is a very difficult relationship; that, to whatever extent it is started in love and blessed by the church, and then perhaps further cemented by the birth of children, it does in fact put at times very great strains on people who in many other circumstances are tolerant, wise, generous, compassionate and perhaps find it easier to show those characteristics to almost anyone other than their spouse.

So I do not find it at all surprising, as an individual, that there is a great need for the Institute of Marital Studies, nor that it has had so much work to do over the years and that it will continue to have such work for many years to come. An American sociologist wrote: 'marriages peter out or pan out'. I am fortunate in that mine has been one that has panned out. But for many, however hard they try, that is not so, and that and all the problems that it brings is a strong and enduring foundation of your work.

But enough of personal observations for me as an individual, a husband and a father. My role here today is to assure you of the continuing goodwill and support of Government to what is now to be known as the Tavistock Institute of Marital Studies.

Professor Dunstan, I can assure you that in the Home Office today we no longer have either fires or firescreens—would that we did. We live instead in a modern building designed by Basil Spence, which has been described—and perhaps this description will strike any of you walking across St. James' Park—as looking like two old ladies with baskets on their heads. Not a bad description, actually. But the fact that you referred to us as your 'firm friend' over the years was very much appreciated. It is a description that I will take back to my Home Office colleagues, and I hope it will remain as true in the years ahead as it has been in the years past.

I very much welcome the emphasis in the papers which will be delivered to you today on the general theme of change. I do not think that the founders of the Family Discussion Bureau in 1948 could have foreseen either the speed of change over the ensuing forty years or its fundamental nature, though they, too, were reacting to changes accelerated by the wartime experience.

This is a time when we are particularly conscious of the stresses and strains which exist in a fast-moving, confident, dynamic society—stresses which show themselves in the breakdown of marriages and relationships, in problems of drugs and alcohol misuse, in outbreaks of disorder and, even most tragically, in problems such as child abuse of which we have heard such a lot this week. There is no simple solution to these problems and certainly no solution which can be found exclusively in terms of government action or legislation, but one thread which is running through many aspects of Home Office policy at the moment is the theme of standards of conduct of self-discipline and self-reliance, of inter-agency co-operation, of the role of the voluntary sector and of the contribution of active citizens. This is where you have a very special part to play.

As you know, it was the Denning Report of 1947 which led to direct Home Office financial support to voluntary organisations in the field of marriage guidance. Let me quote from the report:

> There should be a Marriage Welfare Service to afford help and guidance both in preparation for marriage and also in difficulties after marriage. It should be sponsored by the State but should not be a State Institution. It should evolve gradually from the existing services and societies. It should not be combined with judicial procedure for divorce but should function quite separately from it.

And the quotation continues:

> It should be regarded as a function of the State to give encouragement and, where appropriate, financial assistance to marriage guidance as a form of social service, particularly by grants in aid of the voluntary societies working in this field.

Over the last forty years the Government has seen the flair, dynamism and expertise of the voluntary sector revolutionise the world of marriage guidance, both 'at the sharp end' meeting couples with marriage problems, and in research and training typified by the work of the Tavistock Institute of Marital Studies. It is clear to me that a greater involvement of state bureaucracy would not have produced these results. Organisations such as your Institute have responded flexibly to the needs of ordinary people in painful situations and provided the specialism referred to in the Denning Report.

It is a tremendous tribute to the work of the Institute that it has reached its fortieth birthday having coped so well with all these developments and having emerged as so much of a centre of excellence in its specialist fields of helping couples, in training and consultation and in undertaking research. In doing so, it has demonstrated its relevance to the needs of society and also to the needs of marriage guidance counsellors, therapists, probation officers, social workers, health visitors, solicitors, clergy and the whole range of people whose work involves them in contact with the problems of marital and family stress.

The theme of 'relevance' is one that is well worth lingering on. It is unquestionably important that, in the face of change and stress, support should be available for those families who find it most difficult to cope. I take pleasure in reaffirming the Government's own support for the contribution which the Tavistock Institute of Marital Studies has made in this field. We have been glad to contribute financially to the Institute's work over such a long period—and this contribution is based on our perception of the importance of this work in preserving social stability and in alleviating the personal suffering inherent in family break-up.

But it is vital that any organisation operating in this field should be able to continue to demonstrate, both to members of the public who might want to use its services and to organisations which contribute to its funding, that its work continues to be relevant to the needs of society. In this way it can best demonstrate that it is providing value for the money invested in it. I also suggest that there is a very real danger in becoming too dependent on any one source of funding and in failing to develop the expertise and flexibility necessary to respond to the needs of the market for which you are catering. I am conscious that the use of this language may jar—and I have no wish to spoil a happy occasion—but the Government believes strongly that it is in the interests of voluntary organisations in general—not simply those working in this area—that they should build up a capacity for receptiveness to external needs together with the right measure of self-reliance and internal dynamism.

I have been very pleased indeed to learn how successfully the Institute has risen to this challenge. What is particularly praiseworthy is the way that this challenge is being met while preserving the standards of the Institute's contribution to research, training and practice. In this sense it is all the more appropriate that the organisation should, as from today, be changing its name so as to embody the reference to the Tavistock. I salute the old Institute and the work which it has done over the last forty years. I salute—and bring the good wishes of the Home Secretary and my colleagues at the Home Office to—the new Tavistock Institute of Marital Studies, and I wish the staff and all those associated with it equal success over the next forty years.

The Tavistock Institute of Marital Studies in retrospect

Christopher Clulow

Were you to have picked up your newspapers on this day forty years ago you would have found little overt reference to marriage. *The Times,* alongside news that the Minister of Health, Mr Bevan, was to make available free hearing aids for the deaf, reported in full on the visit of the King and Queen to the Royal Show in York. This evidence of life continuing as normal for the nation's favourite and archetypal marriage must have been a reassuring sign of stability for a people recovering from the ravages of war and embarking on an ambitious programme of social reconstruction through the newly emerging Welfare State.

The *Manchester Guardian* was preoccupied with production targets and working conditions in the coal mining industry. Only a small paragraph provided a chilling reminder of the intensity and consequences of married passion: it recorded that a young Birmingham man had been sentenced to hang for stabbing his wife to death with a penknife.

To get the lowdown on marriage you would have had to turn to your copy of the *Daily Mirror*. There you would have found this human interest story. A heartbroken wife of 25, and I quote: 'took a last look at the smouldering remains that had been her first married home—the one she had scoured and polished for the last six years—and burst into tears. Clinging to her skirts were her three young children. Her husband, a builder's labourer, was not there to comfort her. He was away building houses for other people'. A cautionary tale here, I think, for all of us in the helping professions. You will be glad to know that the local community rallied round. Neighbours formed a relief committee and raised enough money for them to be housed elsewhere, using the slogan 'It might have happened to you!' Fund raisers take note!

Easier, of course, for us as members of the community to respond to a tangible need for bricks and mortar than to invest in something as amorphous as the quality of marriage. Yet a good marriage can provide the kind of support that might prevent a problem developing into a crisis, and a crisis becoming a disaster. Some people do have to shout louder than others to be heard, and what more apposite way for the wife of a builder's labourer to cry for help than through a situation which requires her husband to start building at home. For those of you unfamiliar with the phrases 'unconscious purpose' and 'acting out', regard this as an introductory lesson!

When publicly reported, the private face of marriage often evokes a mixture of hope and disillusionment which can lead to applause, despair or uncontrollable mirth. At around the same time as the report I have described, the *Daily Mirror* (again) placed two news items alongside each other. Under the heading 'Marriage May Bring Cure' it reported that a hotel receptionist was to wed an army major suffering from a terminal illness in the hope of prolonging his life. Next to this was an account of a husband's attempt to divorce his wife on the grounds of cruelty. His three complaints were that she stuck her knees into his back when he was trying to go to sleep, threatened to hit him with a saucepan of hot porridge and told him she hoped he would choke on his breakfast. The line between a good and a bad marriage is clearly very finely drawn! He didn't get his divorce.

It was into this strange and strangely familiar world that our organisation was born. At that time, as now, there was considerable concern about the incidence of marriage breakdown and threats to family stability. More about that later on this morning. Sufficient to say that through the Denning Report of 1947 and the Harris Report of 1948 the government both drew attention to the need for marriage counselling services and made some provision for them to be funded from public sources.

Concern about the stability of marriage and family life pre-dated the war, and had already been registered by the Family Welfare Association, then the oldest and largest voluntary social welfare organisation in the country. Yet their brief was to cater for a wide range of social need, not just marital problems. What was needed was a pioneering and enquiring spirit to take on the challenge. That spirit was embodied in Enid Balint—the name by which most of us know her—and I am delighted that the lady who started it all is here today, forty years on, to celebrate the fruits of her labours, and those of others who started out with her and took over from where she left off.

Enid talked to me about the early days when she was employed by the Family Welfare Association and worked as an organiser for the Citizen's Advice Bureau. Having taken the trouble to learn the War Damage Act inside out she discovered that nobody wanted to know. People were much more interested in talking to her about their personal experiences and relationships than they were about the social benefits to which they might be entitled. Enid was, of course, interested in hearing about these experiences, and no doubt invited the kind of confidences that might not otherwise have been forthcoming. About two things she became convinced: first, behind many practical problems were relationship problems—more specifically, marital problems. Wives might well turn to outsiders for help when they ran out of housekeeping money rather than ask their husbands for more. Money, like sex, could be a 'no go' area for discussion between husband and wife. Second, these marital problems were surprisingly difficult to resolve. Advice and exhortation were next to useless, and obvious solutions were frequently disregarded.

With the support of Ben Astbury, then General Secretary of the FWA, Enid launched an experimental venture which was at first to be called Marriage Welfare, but because of the sense of social failure associated with that name in fact was called the Family Discussion Bureau. The venture was launched on 20 September 1948, and included Lily Pincus, Kathleen Bannister and Doris Bates (as secretary) among the original team of five. The task of this pioneer experiment was fourfold:

1. to provide a service for people seeking help with marriage problems;
2. to devise techniques appropriate to such a service;
3. to evolve a method of training caseworkers;
4. to find out something about the problem of interpersonal relationships as they reveal themselves in marital difficulties.

Such a venture could not be pursued successfully in isolation. The Bureau turned to staff of the Tavistock Clinic and the Tavistock Institute of Human Relations for training and support. Enid has described this period, and I quote, 'like entering a different world, like talking to a different race of human beings'. 'It was the beginning of life for me', she said. And in some ways, that summarises what the unit she formed has been about ever since: trying to help others come alive in themselves and in their relationships. A fruitful marriage, literal as well as figurative, was established with Dr Michael Balint, from whom the Bureau learned the case conference method of exploring what goes on in the substratum of marriage. Dr Jock Sutherland, then Director of the Tavistock Clinic, also played an important part as one of the consultants to the FDB. He was instrumental in bringing about a major organisational change in 1956 when the Bureau became part of the Tavistock Institute of Human Relations.

Reading the published account of the first five years of the FDB (Bannister et al., 1955) I thought how little has changed over forty years. The personal dimensions of the problems people have in getting along with one another stay remarkably constant over time. And there are even suggestions that the social context has not changed as much as we might think. I came across two quotations in particular which caused me to ponder. The first concerned reasons for failure in marriage which, and I quote, 'arises not from lower standards but from higher ones in the sense that couples accept as necessary a level of satisfaction that would have been beyond the hopes of many a century ago'. How many of us have said something remarkably similar in press interviews over the past twelve months? The second begins: 'In our modern society, where equality of the sexes is, at least in theory, the rule .. '.. Those of us working in the Institute know how unequal the relationship between the sexes has been. It has taken forty years and a current staff ratio of two men to every woman to achieve even the semblance of equality!

There have, of course, been changes since those early days when Lily Pincus chaired the unit. The original objectives of the FDB have, to a degree, been met. We do now have a clearer understanding of what takes place between men and women in the intimacy of marriage, the sorts of difficulties they encounter, the pressures their relationships are subject to at different stages of life, and the purposeful nature of many marital problems.

Having developed confidence in a framework for understanding marital difficulties and a method of providing help, the Bureau began training others. A strong link was forged between the FDB and the Probation Service (which at that time did a lot of marital counselling), and I am glad to say that link still exists. The 1960s were particularly fruitful years in which the FDB established a reputation as an advanced training centre. Teaching methods were extended to encompass group relations skills. Staff began to contribute to teaching programmes organised in the Tavistock Clinic. Courses were run in conjunction with university departments. Training Fellowships were set up for students from this country and from overseas foreshadowing the beginning, last October, of the first analytic marital psychotherapy training in the country. Reflecting the increased importance of its role in the study of marriage and the training of practitioners, and wishing to convey more accurately the range and depth of its activities, the FDB was in 1968 renamed the Institute of Marital Studies.

Douglas Woodhouse, who has chaired the unit for seventeen years of its history, presided over this period of change. It was a period in which the Institute established its own monograph series, a series which has gained a reputation for detailed descriptions of the process of working with troubled marriages. He also ushered in the new era in which men, in growing numbers, were to be found joining the ranks of the full-time staff. And he oversaw another organisational transition as the unit moved in 1979 from the Tavistock Institute of Human Relations into the Tavistock Institute of Medical Psychology, the original parent body of both the Tavistock Clinic and the TIHR.

Recent years have seen many developments in the unit, and it is impossible to chronicle them all. Not the least of these has been the development of an action research programme. Janet Mattinson, who was in the chair of the Institute until her retirement last September, has played a particularly important part in this development. Arising from these projects you can now read about working with marital problems in a Social Services department (Mattinson and Sinclair, 1979), about the role of health visitors in preparing couples for the emotional impact of parenthood (Clulow, 1982), about the feasibility of helping divorcing parents reach agreements over child custody and access issues in a welfare enquiry context (Clulow and Vincent, 1987), and about the significance of work—and the loss of work—for couples, and for those employed to help the unemployed (Mattinson, 1988). Training videos are now available about unemployment and marriage and the impact of separation and divorce (TIMS/Rolf Harris video, 1988). Soon you will be able to read about the study of a volunteer telephone helpline service (Colman, 1989), and about the impediments to collaboration between different agencies which cater for the needs of the same families (Pengelly and Woodhouse, forthcoming). In addition to all this, Penguin books will next year be publishing our most up-to-date statement about the insides of marriage under the title *Marriage Inside Out* (Clulow and Mattinson, 1989).

As in the early days, these developments have relied upon partnerships to come to fruition. The partnerships that have taught us the most have been with those who have paid us the compliment of entrusting their relationships to us, the couples who, over the years, have sought our help. We have seldom provided them with solutions to the problems they have brought, but together we have had some success in framing the right questions, clarifying what is at stake and so casting new light on what has perplexed and distressed them within marriage. We have never, in the history of our organisation, faced such a high level of demand for our therapeutic services as we do today. I do not understand why there has been this surge of requests. Maybe some suggestions will be made later on this morning. But I do know that we must respond, as far as we are able, not only through our direct services to couples but also through training and research which assists others, in their own ways, to make an effective response to stress in the family.

Building bridges between different practitioners is no easy task, but it is essential. This week has seen the report of the Butler-Sloss enquiry into alleged child sexual abuse in Cleveland (Butler-Sloss, 1988). It highlights the dilemma facing many of those employed to help families nowadays: how to reconcile pressure from the community to police families, particularly when the interests of children are at stake, and also to provide a personal service which will enhance the capability of those same families to look after their own in their own ways. This is a cruel dilemma. So often it can tempt the professionals to identify only with the parent, or with the child or (in the interests of self-protection) with the community. In the process, two vital elements may get lost. The first is the professional identity of the practitioner, vital if he or she is to play the necessary role of intermediary between conflicting interests within the family and between the family and the community. The second is the relationship of marriage itself—still the heart of family life for the majority of people. The NSPCC reported last month that along with unemployment, marital problems were cited most often as the underlying reasons for child sexual abuse. But in this area, as with the crystallization of so many family issues, marriage is overlooked as a resource that can be mobilised to provide the checks and balances that are so necessary to the healthy development of individuals and families. I am glad that we are participating with the Tavistock Clinic in a project that allows for the couple's perspective to be taken into account when considering the professional response to child abuse and to the creative potential of the differences which exist between practitioners.

Taking less extreme situations, there are important challenges facing the relatively few of us working in the field of marital work. At a recent meeting between the heads of Relate, the Catholic Marriage Advisory Council, Jewish Marriage Guidance, the Marriage Research Centre and ourselves, we asked how we might work together to face the challenges ahead. The challenges are many. How much serious attention is being paid to the relationship between work and the family, those two key areas of life which most of us regard as the foundations of our personal and social identity? As the post-industrial age introduces information technology into the home and requires increasing mobility of a dwindling workforce, what effects will this have on the stability of family life? How will marriage be affected if the employment of women and the unemployment of men continue to grow hand in hand? From what sources will there be help to manage the structural changes which will result from the greying of the population? Answers to these and other large questions will depend in part upon the personal resources people are able to summon up to help them change. And my hope is that this organisation, in partnership with others, will play a growing part in thinking about these social changes, their implications for couples and the process of mutual influence which operates between the inner world of personal experience and the outer world of social and material realities.

In this adventure, our particular contribution is likely to remain firmly rooted in the psychodynamic interpretation of personal and social experience. We value the connections that exist between past and present and which provide a thread of continuity and meaning in life. The past can have a powerful influence upon the present. In my foray into the newspaper archives for 1948 I came across this personal ad: 'Widower, 54, abstainer, needs a very stout, short partner, about the same age or over, same as late wife. Send weight, height and photo. Do not write unless 14 stone or over'. Although the past is powerful—indeed, sometimes weighty—the future cannot be fashioned in its image. Some aspects of the past have to be mourned in order that necessary changes can take place. By valuing the connections between past and present we are concerned to keep in touch with our roots, not to erect a mausoleum.

Our roots have always been firmly in the Tavistock tradition. We have long years of association with the Tavistock Centre, we share a philosophy of life and a framework of beliefs with the Tavistock Clinic and with our parent body the Tavistock Institute of Medical Psychology. We have in common a mission to build bridges in understanding and practice between the wisdom of psychoanalysis and the ordinary experiences of everyday life. We have decided it is time to make 'an honest woman' of ourselves by taking the name 'Tavistock'. On our fortieth anniversary, the Tavistock Institute of Marital Studies welcomes you to celebrate its birthday.

Marriage and social change

David Clark

Change of any sort can be a source of excitement, encouragement and hope. It can also induce fear, anxiety and disillusion. Change in marriage, an institution which is central to so many of the cherished values within our society, is therefore a powerful subject. In the fairly brief space available to me here I want to sketch in some of the main aspects of social change relating to marriage which have occurred over the last forty years. I shall try to show how both the institution and the relationship of marriage inter-connect with a variety of other arrangements, such as the political economy, the law and changes in social and behavioural norms. I want to suggest that an understanding of marriage can never be separated from that of the social context in which it occurs.

Social reconstruction: 1948–59

The years following the Second World War were marked by a preoccupation with the reconstruction of British society, politically, economically and culturally. With the election of a Labour government in 1945 a major series of social reforms ushered in the welfare state, in which medical and social care would be provided 'from the cradle to the grave'. The Family Discussion Bureau, later to become the Institute of Marital Studies, began its work in the same year, 1948, that the National Health Service was founded. The work of the Bureau reflected a new willingness to offer support to those whose family relationships might suffer as a result of social or personal problems.

It was a time of concern about change in marriage. The war was thought to have had a number of adverse effects upon marital and family relations: men away for long periods of time, parents and children separated by evacuation and, no less undesirable in some quarters, women gaining access to traditionally male domains of paid employment in factories and offices. David Mace, in his book *Marriage Crisis,* published in 1948, drew attention in particular to the effects of wartime conditions on sexual morality: 'by the time the six long years were over, our accepted standards of sexual behaviour had slumped very badly' (Mace, 1948:63).

This assessment of the impact of the war on the institution of marriage was supported by the demographic evidence of the period. The years 1946–50 marked the highest ever divorce rate recorded in England and Wales up to that time. At a level of 3.7 divorces per 1,000 of the married population, this was over six times higher than it had been in the years immediately before the war. Marital breakup on that scale was not to occur again for over two decades.

Such trends had no doubt led to the decision to establish a Royal Commission on Marriage and Divorce, which began its enquiries in 1951 with a concern for 'the need to promote healthy and happy married life and to safeguard the interests and well-being of children' (Cmnd. 9678:7, 1956). The commissioners acknowledged that an increased propensity to divorce could be attributable to a variety of factors. Housing scarcities, youthful marriage and the willingness to postpone having children were cited as causes. So, too, were expectations of a higher standard of living and women's economic emancipation. As the report rather ambiguously put it, 'Women are no longer content to endure the treatment which in past times their inferior position forced them to endure' (ibid.:9). Again there was a concern with sexual morality and behaviour; popular psychology was called to task for promoting the interests and personal gratifications of the individual 'without a similar emphasis on the other stable and enduring factors of a lasting marriage' (ibid.:9). Most insidious of all, in the commissioners' view, 'at the root of the problem' was the 'tendency to take the duties and responsibilities of marriage less seriously than formerly' (ibid.:9).

Such public pronouncements served to construct marriage as a social problem, calling for remedies and interventions. In the same year that the FDB began its activities the National Marriage Guidance Council had also been formed, with a set of general principles which included the 'public duty to do everything possible to prevent the tragedy of the broken home, and the train of evils which it initiates, by the provision of sympathetic and expert treatment for the prevention and cure of marital disharmony'. The medical language here is interesting and points to a theme that was to persist in later debates on intervention in marriage: the extent to which marital problems could be defined, codified and made amenable to particular styles of therapeutic intervention.

In fact the marriage guidance movement did much to swing the emphasis away from a medicalised view of marriage problems, in favour of an approach which through the use of trained lay volunteers could offer a client-centred form of *counselling* service. Herbert and Jarvis, in an early work on the subject, state the case for this approach in cautious fashion: 'Marriage counselling in this form is not a substitute for religion nor for legal or medical advice; it is simply a means by which people can be helped to see themselves and their marriages with greater insight—a means by which they can be assisted towards a resolution of their own problems' (Herbert and Jarvis, 1959:21).

Published in 1959 this book struck an important chord, reflecting a growing preoccupation with the internal qualities of the marriage *relationship*. On both sides of the Atlantic sociologists began to interpret this preoccupation as a consequence of the growing *isolation* of the nuclear family from the wider networks of kinship, neighbourhood or the workplace. New ideals of 'companionate' marriage emerged in which the marital relationship was increasingly valued as a source of personal fulfilment and the site of central life interests. Two major studies conducted in London in the late 1950s explored some of the causes and consequences of this. Young and Willmott (1957) described how the marriage relationship could be altered by a range of external factors, such as slum clearance programmes and the development of suburban housing estates, where the breakup of traditional local communities produced new expectations of family-centred lifestyles. Elizabeth Bott (1957) showed how these looser outside networks could produce joint conjugal roles in which husband and wife spent more time together, paid greater attention to the quality of their relationship and sought mutual satisfaction in building a home together.

By the end of the period it was as if public concern about the breakdown of marriage and the family had given way to a new confidence, based on the evidence of social and economic recovery. The process of post-war reconstruction had included family life, and major changes were underway in popular expectations of marriage. From now on quality would take increasing precedence over durability.

Hope and experience: 1960–79

Academic commentaries on marriage in the early 1960s, reflecting these social changes, showed an increasing congruence of sociological and psychological perspectives. Berger and Kellner, in a famous essay written in 1964, described marriage as 'a dramatic act in which two strangers come together and redefine themselves'. Its dominant themes were 'romantic love, sexual fulfilment, self discovery and self realization through love and sexuality'. This is the language of a society buoyed up by economic success, confident in its ability to reformulate old values in new guises. It was the era, *par excellence,* where marriage as institution gave way to marriage as relationship.

The institutional aspects of marriage, family life and sexual relations were progressively deregulated in the 1960s. Briefly we see what Jeffrey Weeks has called 'the permissive moment' (1981: chapter 13). Reforms took place in the laws relating to homosexuality, abortion and censorship. The 1969 Divorce Reform Bill sought to dispense with concepts of 'innocent' and 'guilty' parties to the ending of a marriage. Much influenced by the Church of England report *Putting Asunder,* published three years earlier, the bill made 'irretrievable breakdown' the sole ground for ending a marriage in divorce. With this reform in the divorce law, as Burgoyne, Ormrod and Richards put it, 'the concept of marriage as a partnership has almost been reached. It can be dissolved by the court when it becomes unworkable . . . but it cannot yet be dissolved by the parties themselves' (1987:57).

This deregulation was consistent with changing ideologies of marriage. Liberals argued that it reflected a concern to take marriage *more* rather than *less* seriously. High levels of personal investment in marital happiness implied that when a relationship was found wanting it should be ended without undue constraint and the parties left free to try again with another partner. The interpretation seems to be born out by the social trends. Having fallen in the late 1950s, divorce rates now began to rise; they continued to climb throughout the following decade and by 1979 stood at a rate of 11.2 per 1,000 of the married population. By this time one marriage in three was likely to end in divorce, and a new chapter had been opened in the history of marital relationships in Britain.

If the 1960s was the era of hope, the 1970s was the decade of experience. Mass divorce became a feature of social life, and a range of concerns about its consequences found their way onto the agendas of researchers, practitioners and policy makers. Divorce was shown to be detrimental to health and to the well-being of children; it created pressure on housing, social work and welfare services. But it also assumed a central place within the culture and was no longer seen as the refuge of a deviant minority too fickle or inadequate to sustain a lifelong relationship.

It was during these years that a sea change occurred in our understanding of marriage and family life. Liberal ideas of the companionate marriage came under attack; joint conjugal roles were dismissed as more ideal than real; and the entire system of family divisions based on gender was called into question. Feminism now constituted itself as a major intellectual and political movement which was to bring about significant changes in the coming years. Jessie Bernard (1973) called us to consider the *two* marriages—his and hers—that exist in every marital 'partnership'. A variety of writings, on housework, childcare and patterns of female employment, all pointed to the ways in which marriage may serve to exploit the interests of women. Research evidence went on to reveal the problems of single parents (mainly mothers), and the 'new' social issue of wife abuse was given increasing attention.

Yet despite these darker images, marriage seemed to remain a highly desirable state for one important group: the divorced. By the late 1970s one marriage in three taking place was a remarriage for one or other of the partners. The phenomenon of mass divorce had been joined by that of mass remarriage. We might interpret this as further evidence of the shift away from marriage as institution to marriage as a relationship, largely stripped of its legal, moral and religious significance. When Jackie Burgoyne and I carried out a study of divorced and remarried couples in Sheffield in the late 1970s we went on to entitle our book *Making a Go of It* (Burgoyne and Clark, 1984); the phrase, taken from one of our respondents, echoed the optimistic view that remarriage could be a fresh start, an opportunity to wipe the slate clean and begin a new life with a new partner. But as our work progressed it became clear that remarriage could never be this and that the fresh start is frustratingly baulked by emotional and material legacies from the past, such as custody, access and maintenance arrangements. In this sense marriage has not been stripped of its institutional elements, but continues to carry a variety of obligations, relating to children, property and finance.

Remarriage and the creation of a stepfamily, which so often accompanies it, lead to new, more complex kinship networks that to some extent reverse the pattern of 'isolation' which had been identified in the 1950s. For adults and children alike they present new challenges, of living and growing in settings that are different from what Edmund Leach called 'the cornflakes packet norm' of mum, dad and the two kids.

The 1970s was a decade in which we heard a great deal about the *pluralisation* of family life. Diversity was championed as the new norm in marital and family relations. Everyone should be free to adopt modes of living according to their preference. These ideas were not only articulated by researchers and policy makers, but were also a considerable influence upon those involved in marital therapy and counselling. They form a strong undercurrent to the decade's most significant statement on the work of the marital agencies, *Marriage Matters,* the report of an interdepartmental working party (Home Office, 1979). The report created high expectations, but has led to little action. Its main recommendations for the fostering of better links between research, training and practice in marital work have been slow to develop and the proposal for a Central Development

Unit for marital work has never been taken up. *Marriage Matters'* liberal tolerance for new styles of marriage and new approaches to marital problems strongly reflects the human growth and psychotherapeutic ideologies which had come to surround marriage in the 1960s and 1970s. This concern with internal worlds, processes and dynamics was soon to be called into question in the harsher political and ideological climate of the 1980s.

Social realism: 1980–88

Change in marriage in the 1980s has to be seen in the context of other major upheavals: deep recession followed by economic growth; the widening gulf between conditions in the North and South of Britain; the rise of an enterprise culture and the articulation of 'new right' political ideologies. These cross-cutting political, economic and cultural forces have tended to polarise debates surrounding the family. Ferdinand Mount, for example, has bemoaned the inability of families to function autonomously and to kindle a spirit of independence from state interference, seeing evidence of an over-interfering state producing dependency and eroding enterprise (Mount, 1983). Increasingly, therefore, we must see policies relating to the family in the context of what Wicks calls 'an inter-connected trinity of family, private market and the voluntary sector'. The much-vaunted 'return to Victorian values' has to be regarded in a political context where the significance of social structure and process has been cast aside in favour of a view which gives far greater prominence to the importance of individuals and of families.

Given that expectations of the marriage relationship have changed so much over four decades, this policy seems likely to create further strains on the institution of marriage. When couples and families uncritically assumed major responsibilities for the care of the elderly and the sick, marital relations were defined in more pragmatic and contingent ways. Today, new burdens of care and obligation falling on families are likely to conflict with the notion of marriage as a source of personal fulfilment and of the family as a 'haven in a heartless world' (Lasch, 1977). This might explain in part why rates of divorce have gone on rising, reaching a record high of 13.4 per 1,000 in 1985. The pressures on marriage can also be seen increasingly in relation to wider social and economic issues: divorce rates are lowest among the professional classes, are four times higher among unskilled manual workers and are highest of all among unemployed persons, regardless of class.

At the same time, real rates for first marriage have continued their decline into and through the 1980s, suggesting a greater caution on the part of young people about entering into the state of matrimony. Occurring slightly later, but following the same pattern, rates of remarriage have been falling since 1979. By contrast, cohabitation is becoming more popular: 24% of women marrying for the first time between 1979–82 had cohabited with their husbands beforehand, and where one or other of the partners was remarrying the proportion was 65%. Most striking of all have been rises in the illegitimacy rates; 22% of babies born in the first nine months of 1987 were 'non-marital', in the language of recent legislation. Moreover, about two-thirds of these babies are registered by both parents, suggesting that they are born into relatively stable non-marital relationships.

It is too early to predict where these changes might lead, and we must remind ourselves that in recent decades marriage has been more popular than at any other point in our history; but these trends may just provide evidence of some secular social movement away from a preoccupation with marriage as the normative basis for adult relationships. Indeed, the 1980s have also reminded us that significant numbers of adults within our society actively seek out alternatives to heterosexual relationships. One of the few silver linings in the tragic history of the AIDS epidemic may yet be the extent to which it allows gay and lesbian relationships to be recognised as authentic alternatives to heterosexual love and marriage. To that extent the legal deregulation of marriage has been accompanied by similar processes in the cultural and moral spheres.

In the late 1980s marriage seems uneasily poised. It has clearly undergone massive social change over the past four decades. These changes may be interpreted in a variety of ways. Whether our position is one of disillusion or hope will depend on a variety of factors. One thing seems certain. Forty years on from the opening of the Family Discussion Bureau, the debate about change in marriage needs to come out of the by-ways of academic and therapeutic organisations to occupy a far more central place on the current political and policy-making agenda.

Marriage and personal change

Robin Skynner

It is a great privilege and pleasure to be asked to speak on this happy occasion of the fortieth anniversary of the IMS. I have benefited greatly myself from its pioneering research—their work forms an essential base for my own work and writings, including the popular book, *Families and How to Survive Them* (1983), that John Cleese and I wrote together—and I know of no other centre which opens its doors in the same way not only to share its discoveries with other colleagues working in the field, but to invite their criticism and give opportunities for them to exchange with each other. It is typical that they should use this celebration of their anniversary to encourage an exchange among us in which we can all benefit from the experience and wisdom brought together in this distinguished gathering, and perhaps share some thoughts about what we have to do next.

There were various ways I could have used this limited time, but it seemed most useful to focus on the main theme and ask whether something hopeful might be emerging in a personal sense from a time when marriage and the family have seemed very threatened. In particular, I have responded to the invitation, first, 'to speak informally from my experience' rather than presenting a scientific paper and, second, 'to make some comment about why it might be that there has been a change in conceptual emphasis in regard to marriage and the family', a question I found more interesting the more I thought about it.

Breakdown of old order

There is increasing concern at the effect on marriage and the family of what has appeared, at least on the surface, to be a progressive breakdown in the structure of society. In the western world over the past forty years our values have become increasingly individual—rather than group-centred, swinging the balance away from social cohesion towards personal freedom, often regardless of its social consequences. We have been losing the concept of duty, role, place in society; and of authority and order, including the former influential roles of the father, the extended family and the community. There has been a decline in the influence of religion, in the force of social expectation and in respect for law.

One consequence of this lack of structure is that couples are no longer held and supported through periods of difficulty. We have been losing the idea that creating a marriage is work—even if that work is normally made worthwhile by much pleasure—and that it takes effort and struggle, self-denial, patience, tolerance, kindness and generosity—mixed of course with plenty of humour and fun—to build an enduring relationship. Where before couples might have matured and become strengthened through struggling to overcome their difficulties—'cooked', as it were, by the heat of conflict, they can now more easily jump out of the frying-pan of one relationship into the fire of another similar one just when the stress they are escaping from may be signaling that beneficial developmental changes were about to take place.

Emergence of new forms of relationship

However, at the same time as these degenerative changes in society have been occurring overtly, the seeds of new integrations have been forming in the background and growing in influence. In preparing this talk I became much more clearly aware than before of how we have been going through the painful transition between an old type of order and a new, emerging one. The old type of order is more hierarchical, paternalistic, with authority centred on the leader, and draws mainly on left-brain thinking. The new order is more organic and holistic, drawing on the intelligence of the whole system, including the resources and managerial qualities of both men and women, and with a better balance of right as well as left-brain functioning. The idea that governments know and people do not, that management knows and the work-force does not, that teachers know and pupils do not, that men know and women do not, is giving way to an understanding that the group-as-a-whole has an intelligence far beyond that of any of its members, including the leader(s), and that it is the leaders' main task not to dictate and direct, except in times of crisis, urgent action and otherwise unresolvable conflict, but mainly to nurture and facilitate the group process and resources.

This change towards a new way of thinking is represented in forms of medicine, traditional and alternative, which consider the whole person, treating bodily, mental and spiritual needs together and in a social context; in increasing concern for the environment and awareness of ecological consequences; and in a greater feeling of responsibility for world conditions, evidenced at one extreme by vast spontaneous movements arising from younger people and sharing a common goal of helping others in dire need, as for instance the extraordinary phenomenon of 'Band-Aid'. And at the other, there is increasing co-ordination of financial policy through summit meetings of world leaders and financial institutions, thereby avoiding many disasters that would have happened in the past, however partial and limited in scope such co-operation at present may seem.

New ways of thinking about relationships

This widening of our field of awareness has been reflected in our understanding of personal relationships, including those within marriage and the family. In our own professional work I would see three developments as particularly relevant to our changed understanding. These are: Object-Relations Theory; Attachment Theory; and General Systems Theory.

The early development of both psychoanalysis and learning theory was based on individual-centred thinking, looking at and treating each person separately, one-at-a-time, in isolation. Object-relations theory placed the human individual back into a social context, as part of a network of relationships which influences and sustains us throughout life. Once the group was established in our model of the inner world, it inevitably led some practitioners to take the next step and experiment with the living group itself. Foulkes, Bion, Balint and other psychoanalysts began to explore the actual interaction of groups, watching the intermeshing of the members' projected inner worlds and discovering powerful new forms of treatment in the process. Others, including Bowlby, Dicks and many members of the Institute of Marital Studies, brought together marital partners and other family members to learn about the structure of their inner worlds not just by questioning or listening to the free association of patients about their family relationships, but by watching the interaction at first-hand.

Attachment theory, as developed by Bowlby and his colleagues from its basis in animal ethology, has gone far towards providing an objective, scientific base for this different way of thinking, by systematic and detailed studies of the interaction of parent and child from birth. This research has made us much more aware of the fundamental role of the family and of other social support-systems throughout life. It long ago completely transformed the care of young children needing hospitalization and threatened by separation from parental care, all over the world, and I was pleased to be able to help implement some of its recommendations about mothers' visiting and living-in with their children twenty years ago at the Queen Elizabeth Hospital for Children. I have also now recently experienced the beneficial effects of attachment theory first-hand, on the receiving end as it has been so marvellously applied at the other end of life in the hospice movement, and I cannot find words to describe what a difference its application makes to the happiness and quality of life of both the dying person and the partner. In these and in other ways, attachment theory has created a new climate of opinion in making us more aware of the social context of all our behaviour.

Systems theory, which had its origins in the late 1940s from such sources as Weiner's *Cybernetics* (1948), the *Information Theory* of Shannon and Weaver (1949), and the *Games Theory* of von Neumann and Morgenstern (1947), has developed its tremendous influence over the four decades we are considering. Initially it had a greater influence in the United States and has reached us, or at least reached the mental health professions in this country, indirectly through the American family therapy movement. But in Britain we understood and were applying much of it already—the first paper I know of on family therapy was published here, by Dr Bowlby, in 1949, and when I used to tell my teacher S. H. Foulkes about these new American developments he would usually dismiss them and say 'But that's group analysis'. He was indeed doing it already, from an intuitive understanding, but systems theory provided a new language, and a clearer framework of thought, which illuminated what we were doing and enabled us to see new connections so that we could understand and do it better. Where the knowledge has been applied it has transformed the outlook for the treatment of psychological disorder.

Responsibility in relationships

Despite the costs of increased marital break-up, many have been released by the more relaxed divorce laws and attitudes from what might in the past have been a life-time of bitter conflict and misery. For many others this greater freedom has made life richer and more interesting, opening the way to new levels of growth and relationship. In days when many marriages were more like a business contract—a pay-packet and security exchanged for cooking, sex and housework—divorce could be seen as a failure of the business, or a wrong choice of business partner.

But today the agenda is often based more on mutual growth. A life-long commitment is probably the most growth-facilitating situation of all, provided there is an equal commitment to change. Divorce often indicates that one partner has grown, or wants to grow, more or differently than the other, and that this difference is irreconcilable. Some marriages are like a stage of a journey, where each partner is travelling to a different destination and they move on to other relationships when they have helped each other grow through the appropriate stage. Though I cannot help feeling a warm romantic glow when some couples I see end by walking off into the sunset hand-in-hand, some of those which end in amicable divorce and loving co-operation over care of the children can appear almost equally positive when seen from this point of view.

I have not found in my work that people are in general becoming less responsible about their relationships, as I understand the word 'responsibility'. The more one's behaviour towards others is regulated by rules, by law and social expectation, the more irresponsible one's behaviour is likely to be when there is no-one around and one is distant from one's own doorstep. By contrast, a relaxation in external controls *can* lead to worse behaviour in some, but also to better behaviour in others. Since the social changes of the 1960s I never cease to be impressed by the extraordinary responsibility and care young people in intimate relationships show towards one another, compared with the attitude common at the time of my own youth and young adulthood, and in many older people I see who were brought up in that time.

My colleague Margaret Robinson, who pioneered our conciliation service at the Institute of Family Therapy, pointed out to me how there is now far more negotiation, during courtship or cohabitation and before a final commitment, about issues that in the past would have led to problems at a later stage. For example, couples work out mutually satisfactory agreements about separate friendships with the same or opposite sex early on, instead of entering into marriage with idealised notions of meeting all each other's needs, and then suffering a violent breakdown of this pattern when at midlife one spouse has an affair. There is less illusion built into the relationship, and so the disillusion is less, or it occurs in time to call the relationship off. Stepfamilies in particular are leading the way in this process of negotiation at an early stage, and exploring such issues in a way that will ultimately benefit us all.

The sexual relationship

Another major change affecting personal relationships in marriage has been the enormous increase in knowledge of the range of human sexual behaviour, and in discovering ways to help couples to improve the quality of their lovemaking. Kinsey published *Sexual Behavior in the Human Male* in the year the FDB was founded—1948—and his *Sexual Behavior in the Human Female* followed five years later, in 1953. I remember the profoundly liberating effect it had on all those I knew who read it at the time, as well as upon myself. Whatever the limitations of that research, it opened up this taboo area to more open discussion and scientific study. About half-way through this period Masters and Johnson's publication of *Human Sexual Response* in 1966, and *Human Sexual Inadequacy* in 1970, was another milestone towards a scientific understanding of human behaviour, opening the way to modern rapid treatments of sexual dysfunctions. The skills are widely distributed among professionals in clinics and hospitals, and throughout the country the former Marriage Guidance Councils—or Relate, as they have since been renamed—now have 101 such clinics operating.

These studies attracted great public interest and were widely publicized in the media. The relaxation of taboos on the publication of sexual material made this information available to all, in best-selling books like *The Joy of Sex* (Comfort, 1974), giving permission for couples to discuss their sexual difficulties, and enough help for some to overcome them without need for professional help. Although this greater freedom of communication was inevitably abused by some, and although it produced new anxieties where couples feared they might not be 'keeping up with the Jones's' in their orgasm tally, it is my impression that this increased openness and relaxation on the topic of sexuality has been of great benefit towards improving the quality of married life and of family happiness.

Changes in the roles of women and men

These changes in sexual attitude are just one aspect of the tremendous change that has occurred over this period in the way women perceive their feminine role, whether or not they have belonged to the women's movement in any formal way or even support it consciously. In the couples I have seen during this time the women have shown a steadily greater confidence, a more solid sense of personal identity, an increasing demand for personal freedom, for equality, for a greater measure of independence and right to their own separate lives, for an equal share in the partnership of marriage, and for at least a fairer deal, even if not an exactly equal deal, as regard child-care and housework. Increasingly, in the troubled couples I see it is the women who have been calling the shots, initiating divorce, having affairs.

The expansion in the self-image of women was potentially liberating for men, who were equally locked into restricted patterns of behaviour by social expectation. Men have benefited from engaging in the change too, and I am certainly grateful to feel so much more relaxed and free now than my father or my grandfather appeared to be, or than I did myself when I was young. But in general the male sex has been slow to follow the women's initiative, and men have tended either to dig in and resist the changes in women, or to follow their demands too slavishly (this second, too conciliatory reaction appearing to infuriate them even more than the first!). What seems to be needed is for men to continue to be men, different and separate, but to engage in the process and learn from it.

This change can be observed regularly in the couples' groups I run, and which my wife and I have worked with together for over sixteen years. To start with, the women are intensely frustrated and attack the men in oblique ways, but at the same time they inhibit themselves as if fearful of destroying the male self-esteem, which they perceive as fragile and likely to collapse if not buttressed by their support. There seems to be no conditioning so powerful as that which inhibits a woman from criticizing a man in ways that would really threaten his confidence in his male sexual role. However, if the woman is supported in sustaining her attacks, and the man in taking her criticisms on board, eventually he begins to engage in the dialogue in a more forthright, open and constructive way. Often he will seize the initiative and then take the lead for a time, but eventually they achieve a more equal relationship, embodying mutual respect for each other's strengths and becoming a match for each other. I believe this kind of struggle now has to be worked out at a social level.

Research on exceptionally healthy families

Finally, the most hopeful development of all has been the research into exceptionally healthy families, which has been available for only the last of our four decades. When I first went to train at the Maudsley near the beginning of this period, in 1953, I searched the library there for references to papers about mental health—by which I mean optimal health, exceptional health in the sense that olympic athletes are exceptionally athletic. I found only three: two contained little of interest and the third was impressionistic, though it contained unexpected findings and whetted my appetite. It was another twenty years before information about really healthy individuals, couples and families—for example, that of the Timberlawn Research Foundation in Texas (Lewis et al., 1976), and Vaillant's (1977) report of the Grant Study on the health of Harvard graduates over forty years—began to fill this gap.

There are several very hopeful aspects of this research. Many of the qualities these families show are those that common sense would lead us to expect, like warmth, openness, trust, mutual respect, responsibility and neighbourliness. But some findings are rather unexpected; in some ways they seem able to have their cake and eat it, in that the members are very independent and can enjoy separate lives and do without each other, yet can also be unusually close and intimate, with the parents usually showing a pattern of long-term marital fidelity. Far from being dull, such families are unusually lively, spontaneous, playful and amusing.

All the ideas I have outlined earlier are helpful towards understanding why such families function well; for example, their strengths required a capacity to deal resiliently with change and loss, including the death of loved ones, and this in turn depended on powerful support systems, including a sense of one's place and connection with the cosmos. This knowledge is helpful whatever one's own level of health, because it gives us a direction to aim for.

Changing marriage

Barbara Dearnley

I have been trying to believe in and relish Oscar Wilde's statement that 'on an occasion of this kind it becomes more than a moral duty to speak one's mind. It becomes a pleasure'. But with so many in this audience from whom I have gratefully learnt my trade, it is not easy to be so confident. I also have reservations about that part of my given title which hints omnipotently at the TIMS holding the secret of change, or therapy being a panacea for changing marriage; neither I nor the TIMS would lay claim to that. Such perhaps may be the disillusioning but realistic part of what I have to say today.

As marital psychotherapists we work within a forty-year old institution that has itself been changing. I joined the Family Discussion Bureau (as it then was) in 1960, and in these 28 years I have seen the staff of the unit change from predominantly female to predominantly male, from a majority of part-timers to a very largely full-time staff. When I joined, all workers had to be married and psychiatric social workers—though being an analyst might do! I saw the first milestones of an unmarried worker recruited from other branches of social work, our first change of name to describe our function more accurately, and the first step in charging clients when we could no longer survive without fees. I saw the departure of our founding mothers—Enid Balint, Lily Pincus, Kathleen Bannister. We moved from appallingly cramped conditions in central London to a new, purportedly purpose-built, roomier Tavistock at Swiss Cottage. During those years I lived through four Chairman 'reigns'—Lily Pincus, Douglas Woodhouse, Janet Mattinson and now Christopher Clulow—who, as Douglas would say, 'were horses for courses', reflecting in themselves the unit's need for different leaders at different times. I have learnt much from them all and think we have been most fortunate in our horses—Grand National, Derby, Cheltenham Gold Cup and 2000 Guinea winners all. I will resist elaborating on who are the steeple-chasers, the flat runners and what weight they carry!

Through all these different reigns—which have had more of the equestrian sense of reigning in and harnessing unbridled individual enthusiasms than any sense of sovereignty—the Institute has existed to bring about change; not in the reformist sense of imposing change from the outside, but through seeking to understand why change is often so difficult to accomplish and creating the conditions in which it can become a less frightening prospect than it so often is. That said, the work also has to embrace living with what cannot be changed, and that is no mean feat.

There are many factors that bring about change in marriage. Social and economic circumstances have a powerful influence. It makes a difference if young couples can have a place of their own to live in rather than share with parents, if there are employment opportunities to relieve money worries and provide a structure and purpose, and if the laws of the land and the views of its people do not discriminate between men and women. The passage of time and what life holds in store for people also make an impact. The arrival of children, or the failure of children to arrive when they are keenly wanted, challenges the resources of a marriage. So, too, does the toll exacted by sickness, handicap and death of those dear to the couple—especially children. The dazzling career of one partner may be at the expense of the other, and the loss of job will also have serious implications for marriage (see Mattinson, 1988). In Janet Mattinson's words, the businesses of 'making a living' and 'making a loving' are closely intertwined. But it is not just life events that determine what happens to marriage, it is what people make of these events. And this human factor introduces an infinite variety of possibilities.

There is not the time for me to expand on these broad themes this morning. Instead I want to make four brief points about the potential of therapeutic help to change marriages. While I shall be drawing on our specific experience in our unit, I believe that what I have to say will be relevant to others here today who offer services to families but who are not marriage specialists. So here, hopefully, is the condensed wisdom of forty years about the ingredients that determine how far it is possible to change marriage through a helping therapeutic relationship.

These are the four ingredients:

1. What people expect their marriage to do for them.
2. What couples expect of those who offer professional help.
3. The response couples receive upon asking for help.
4. The nature of the organisational base from which such services are offered.

The first factor affecting the potential for change concerns what people expect their marriages to do for them. Those of you here who are historians could debate about the relative importance of the economic, social and emotional ties that have bound couples together at different times in history.

From my more limited historical perspective I think we see a greater proportion of disillusioned (or should I say realistic?) couples in the 1980s than before. Now couples often want to make hard-bitten decisions about whether to stay together or part, or to assess whether their relationship will withstand a child; whereas in the 1960s and early 1970s rising expectations could motivate a search for a better quality of relationship as an end in itself. But now, of course, it is easier to decide to leave a marriage. And that makes a difference.

Unmarried couples accounted for 15% of people seeking our help last year; 41% of the total had no children, and 28% were remarriages for one or both partners. The first publication from the FDB (Bannister et al., 1955) records no details of unmarried or remarried couples seen between 1949 and 1953, but it does record that only 12% then had no children. Moreover, while it is now couples in their thirties and forties who are most likely to come to us, the balance then lay in the 20–30 age group. This is not simply a reflection of people now marrying later, but a real difference between those who contacted the FDB when their marriages were relatively young, and those who now contact us, two-thirds of whom have been married for more than ten years.

Whatever this means about changing patterns and expectations, some expectations of marriage remain fundamentally unchanged. All of us continue to need and search for security and fulfilment through our intimate relationships with that special other person. In Jock Sutherland's words: 'everybody needs to be somebody's somebody'. Unfinished business from childhood, unsatisfied emotional longings, unmet physical needs, generate hopes and fears which are carried into our adult relationships and especially into marriage. In a timeless introduction to the first FDB textbook on marriage, Geoffrey Thompson described marriage as 'the most direct heir of the intense primary relationships of childhood', going on to observe that: 'the experiences of the early years go far to determine, in conjunction with the nature of the child's hereditary endowment, the kind of adult into which he may grow, the kind of beliefs he will have about himself and other people, the kind of personal relationships he will be able to form with them, and the extent to which he will be able to fulfil his inherent biological and psychological potentialities, upon the fulfilment of which the satisfactoriness and "worthwhileness" of his life so largely depend' (Pincus, 1960). These beliefs and expectations are modified by our experiences of others throughout life, and not least through our 'other half'—be they a better or worse half—in marriage. Disillusion is therefore part of the proper experience of marriage, freeing us to engage with others as they really are rather than how we would like them to be. The degree of rigidity with which illusions are maintained in a marriage therefore has a close bearing on how far it is possible to change marriage.

The second factor affecting the potential for change concerns what couples expect of those who are there to help. The processes of therapy are often a mystery to outsiders, and no doubt we could do better in conveying something about the experience of seeking and (hopefully obtaining) help. This is, however, a very individual and unpredicatable business.

Despite a growing climate of openness it is still much more difficult to acknowledge a marital problem than an individual problem. Although mixed feelings are always involved, it is easier to seek help for oneself as a parent in difficulties with children than it is to go for help about one's own marriage. Marriage is a very private affair: it is intimately connected with our need for security and hopes of being loved. To seek help in this sphere of life may raise fears of things being said which might be better left unsaid, of learning that which one would have preferred not to know, and of facing the prospect either of feeling trapped in marriage or ejected from it.

Just as there are conscious and unconscious hopes and fears entertained in marriage, so there are conscious and unconscious expectations of therapy. The motivation for seeking help to change marriage may be less strong than a desire to establish that he is to blame or that she needs treatment, to move backwards into the past rather than forwards into a different kind of relationship, or to *seem* to be doing something about a bad situation in order not to do anything about it at all. But what is sure, is that unconsciously the essence of the problem with which a couple is trying to tangle will be reconstructed in the helping relationship in the hope that, there, it can be managed differently and lead to change. This unconscious expectation of the clients needs to be met consciously by the therapists.

I will briefly illustrate what I mean. Chris and I saw a couple some years back who came to us at a time when they felt their relationship was at a crossroads: either they were to make a commitment to each other and start a family or they were to go their separate ways. The husband, Bill, wanted children; the wife, Ruth, did not. Their sexual relationship, once so good, was ailing.

They spoke of an unbridgeable gulf in their emotional inheritance. Ruth came from a family of girls where the parents were happily married, the father successful and the family admired. She, however, was father's favourite, seeking to emulate his success. She still felt that she would have made her father a better wife than her mother did. Her father had recently died and the family had turned to her for help and support. They seemed to reinforce her role as father's deputy. In contrast, Bill went back three generations to illustrate a continuing inheritance of unhappiness and disappointment in family life. His mother, though lively, was very demanding of his time and attention. His parents constantly warred with each other and, as the only child, Bill felt obliged to mediate between them. His father was ailing, unable to work, and Bill was convinced his father would eventually drink and smoke himself into an early grave.

So it seemed that our couple was burdened with a legacy from fathers who were either dead and distinguished, or just alive and disappointing. Ruth had been unable either to give up her father sufficiently to commit herself to Bill, or to come to terms enough with her mother to contemplate becoming a mother herself. Bill had to live up to the reputation of his father-in-law and live down that of his own father. Moreover, he had to overcome the sense that Ruth and his mother were one and the same person when struggling with his own feelings of failing to measure up.

We worked with Ruth and Bill for over a year, mourning lost and dying fathers and living with their growing anger and reproach as they exposed their fear that neither would be a dependable parent to the baby they were so ambivalent about giving life to—within themselves as well as in reality. In the course of this process I found myself in the uncomfortable position of being the therapist each wanted and competed for. Chris said he felt redundant, but admiring of my interpretations and lively work, wondering how he was going to compete—should he fight his way in, or give up and take to the bottle! Rivalry loomed for us as it did for the couple.

We were saved from replicating the envious attacks and quarrelsomeness of the couple by our knowledge of unconscious processes. We knew we had been allowed to experience at first hand something of what it felt like to be in their shoes, and that this communication was as important as anything which had been expressed in words. With this knowledge we could allow the therapeutic experience to be a little different from what, unconsciously, they were engineering. Chris resisted the temptation to take personally their preference for me and so did not retaliate by fighting with or distancing himself from either me or them. I resisted the temptation to become Mother Earth and continued to feel and express my need and valuing of Chris. In that way I believe we disappointed the outcome that past history had led them to expect. By enabling our partnership—the therapists' parental marriage—to survive them, we fulfilled some of their hope in us that we could give them a different experience. For every appeal for help contains the hope for change: as therapists we keep alive that hope.

The marriage changed. Fathers were talked about in less idealised or denigrated terms. Mothers gained in value but managed not to be put on pedestals. Rivalry and feelings of rage abated, intimacy became less feared, sex slowly revived and contraception was given up. The last we heard of them was from their own spontaneous follow up—a card announcing the birth of a son, the death of a father and Bill's promotion at work.

Having talked about people's expectations of marriage and their hopes of therapy, I have now moved into the third area which is highly relevant to the therapeutic possibilities for changing marriage: the response that a couple receives upon asking for help. It seems to me that this has two components: firstly, the knowledge and skill of the practitioner—that is, the mixture of personal and professional experience she or he brings to the helping relationship and the willingness to be influenced as well as to influence—and, secondly, the structuring of the helping relationship. These components need to be well-married.

Taking the last point first, that of structure: at the TIMS we provide couples with two therapists, regular weekly meetings for an hour and the possibility of separate as well as joint meetings. In other words, we do our best to provide a predictable but flexible environment in which couples can undertake therapy, which is properly a journey of exploration. Twenty years ago, Alison Lyons wrote a paper for a book celebrating fifty years of the Tavistock Clinic in which there was an account of one therapy where the husband and wife were seen separately throughout (Lyons, 1973). Today couples are seen very much more together than apart. Although the balance has changed, the structure reflects dilemmas that are central to marriage: the conflict between needing to be together and to have time apart, the longing for intimacy and the fear of being engulfed, the wish to be the same as others and the drive to be different, the push for change and the pull of security. As Alison would say, 'every marriage needs its garden shed'—as well as its sitting room.

And, similarly, as a client said to Lily Pincus, 'you must help us to separate us so that we can stay together'.

And that is true of marital therapists in their relationships with couples. We both need to be able to enter into the experience of those who consult us, and to do this we need to have a separate place to stand so that we can bring a different perspective to bear. Entering into the world of couples can be uncomfortable, as I have already indicated. The feelings of failure that couples experience when their marriages go awry can easily be transferred to those who help them, in much the same way as happened in the case of Ruth and Bill. The question for us is whether we can tolerate and contain such feelings until such time as those who consult us can afford to take them back or whether, in our enterprise culture, which places such a high premium on success, we feel compelled to demonstrate our therapeutic potency. Performance anxiety is not the exclusive domain of those with sexual problems!

The chief safeguard against such anxiety is a secure professional identity. This provides, if I may use the concept that has been so fruitfully developed by John Bowlby, the secure base from which it becomes safe to venture out. Without such a base, venturing out becomes hazardous and we risk getting lost. It is here that training, consultation and professional support has an active role to play. Training for helping people change their relationships is not a one-off enterprise, but a process which needs to be fostered throughout a working career. As with marriage, professional development atrophies with neglect. But so often it is the area in which short cuts and economies are made.

Professional identity includes a clear sense of role, an appropriate body of theoretical knowledge, a coherent philosophy and system of beliefs, and technical competence. One aspect of our professional identity in this unit which I believe works for change by instilling hope in those who consult us, is a belief that conflict has a potential for good as well as ill. If I may refer back to an early FDB book (Pincus, 1960):

> There is no such thing, outside the realms of imagination, as a marriage that is free from conflict. Such a relationship is not in the nature of human beings. In the depths of our minds we never, throughout all our lives, succeed in freeing ourselves fully from the hates and resentments that first arose in infancy, or from the excessive and unreal demands and expectations of those earliest years. . . . The truth is that love and hate are inevitably linked, and a happy and satisfactory marriage is certainly not one that is free from conflict and hate.

The concept of a secure base has considerable institutional implications. And here I move to my fourth, and final, point about the institutional underpinning needed for services aiming at bringing about change. Thanks to the kind of contribution made by Isobel Menzies (see, for example: *The Functioning of Social Systems as a Defence against Anxiety*, 1970) we have become increasingly aware of the connections between what happens in organisations and what happens in the lives of those who constitute the organisation's clients. Work within our own organisation, as well as with social workers, marriage guidance counsellors, probation and divorce court welfare officers, health visitors, the clergy and solicitors has taught us that the nature of the client's difficulties can unconsciously permeate into practice, into attitudes towards supervision and professional support, and into working relationships both within and between organisations. Our experience of working within these different settings confirms Isobel Menzies' statement that 'the success and viability of a social institution are intimately connected with the techniques it uses to contain anxiety.'

For example, the anxiety generated by children at risk and the public role, accountability and front-line position of Social Service departments may too easily shape a crisis response. If the institution responds in a crisis fashion, then the worker is likely so to deal with the client, and the client in turn expects only a first-aid service. Thus the circle is complete and the agency becomes labelled as a casualty service staffed by casualty workers and never dealing with the underlying problems.

In my training hat I have been fortunate to teach—and learn—in an inner London Social Service department that has understood such action and reaction and has also understood that institutions become affected by their primary task and by the nature of their clients' problems. This Social Service department seeks in its understanding and practice to mediate these forces, to contain anxiety and promote the quality of practice. Regular, dependable, technical and supervisory support for all workers at all levels goes far to ensure that the institution is not split, that the temptation to blame and scapegoat is minimised and that 'burn-out' is held at bay. Institutions—and society—need to understand that professional judgement is acquired slowly over time and represents an investment in care to the community requiring the institution's protection and nurture. The worker's capacity to remain open and receptive to clients depends not only on personal and professional qualities, but on the institution's ability to be open, receptive and supportive to its workers. Within the TIMS, I have valued most a working culture where there is freedom to share one's ignorance and mistakes, to be unknowing, and to expose work without fear of being persecuted with advice or criticism. In short, to let one's petticoat show (I think I can be allowed my feminine metaphor on this male platform!).

We can all get caught up in behaving too parentally; pressure is exerted by client on practitioner and by practitioner on managers to become pseudo parents, and, indeed, some risky situations require control. Both practitioners and managers are capable of acting like controlling parents without prompting from outside. But we may all be invigorated to discover that it is unnecessary to over-ride the autonomy of others. A partnership is possible in which people can be encouraged to work out their own solutions and in doing so develop in their relationships. This applies with organisational families as well as between practitioners and families and within families themselves. Such partnerships can be hard to sustain, but I believe the struggle to keep them alive and well is the key to bringing about change in marriages through therapeutic help.

Reactions and comment

A preoccupation with three different relationships pervaded the discussion following the papers:

the relationship between men and women,
the relationship between work and home,
the relationship between public funds and personal services.

Could a hopeful marriage be effected in these areas, or did the future portend disillusion?

Men and women

The opening question concerned the fragility of male self-esteem and how this might be understood. Why was it that women were so successfully conditioned by men (without the process being consciously known about) into not pushing them very hard? Experience of couples in groups suggested that 'pushing' could lead to an escalating process which culminated in an often violent flare-up, but which then resulted in change between the couple and an improved relationship. An anxiety about putting men under pressure was expressed by a woman who commented on the risk of men dying of coronary heart disease between the ages of 45 and 55; this was a dilemma for women who felt themselves getting stronger but feared standing up for themselves. Heart disease (or perhaps a disease of the heart?) seemed to be where men were vulnerable.

This theme was returned to later in the discussion where research was cited in which boys had proved more vulnerable than girls to the impact of parental divorce. Perhaps education was needed to revise cultural 'macho' stereotypes of manhood so that masculinity could encompass feelings, needs and relatedness. How far did the culture of today reinforce male tendencies to deny needs and feelings and to escape from the world of domesticity and emotions at home through becoming 'action men' at work?

Work and home

One participant spoke about her work in industry helping companies to increase and develop their female resources. The relationship between work and the family was of key importance. It could be the source of considerable stress through people having divided loyalties, and the time had come to bring the debate into the public arena. Statements about Victorian values contained conflicting messages about the proper place of men and women. It was important to mitigate conflict in this area and put the 'balanced lives' issue for men and women on management agendas.

One contributor spoke of the favourable climate now existing for taking forward the work/home debate. From his perspective in industry there was a very real danger that good, thoughtful and balanced people in industry would forgo promotion in order to give priority to their personal and family relationships. This could create a crisis of governance in industry and was one reason why companies might be interested in the knowledge and skills possessed by family organisations. The quality of non-working life was becoming an increasingly important consideration. What was lacking was the connection between those working to improve the quality of life at home and those working to improve the quality of life at work. To make this connection might, incidentally, remove some of the financial anxiety experienced by family organisations. The transfer of a very small slice of what is currently being spent on improving functioning at work would very significantly increase funds for those currently working on the home front.

Counterbalancing this argument was the evidence that between fifty and sixty companies had been invited to send representatives to the conference, and only a tiny minority had accepted. The case for making connections was unassailable; putting it into practice was more difficult. The experience of one speaker who had studied the family life of those working on oil rigs in the North Sea provided evidence of stress generated by different patterns of work, but also of a clash of cultures and values which was extraordinarily difficult to mediate.

Public resources and personal services

Feelings ran highest in the discussion about government policy towards service agencies. Commenting on the gentle reception given to the Minister, one participant said 'let us not feed the hand that bites us'. What impact had the enterprise culture had on the operations of TIMS, for example?

Picking this question up specifically, and with others responding from their organisational viewpoint, it was recognised that up to a point the challenge to earn and innovate could be productive and result in initiatives that might otherwise not have been taken. However, it could stultify initiative if survival anxiety became too high, diverting organisations from their proper purpose and breeding self-interested competitiveness rather than co-operation and interdependence. Government policy provided an environment that affected how organisations operated. Insidiously, changes were occurring in which only those who could afford to pay received service. The personal services were in danger of being devalued in favour of commercial activity.

Evidence was given of a drift of certain kinds of client away from statutory organisations (which could no longer afford to provide some personal services) towards the private, fee-charging sector. TIMS had temporarily had to stop accepting referrals for marital therapy (where fees are charged according to ability to pay), and this high level of demand was also being experienced by Relate (Marriage Guidance) in London where the waiting list for counselling was currently 800 strong. Lack of resources could lead organisations down paths that would not normally be taken simply in order that they might survive to fight another day.

Appreciation was expressed for Mrs Dearnley's comments about the institutional support necessary for servicing practitioners in the field. The danger at present was that many organisations offering personal services were beleaguered and unable to fulfil these basic requirements, resulting in anti-therapeutic stances and attitudes. Practitioners might then operate paternalistically, or politicise their behaviour, becoming standard bearers with or for their clients. Privatisation was linked with the profit motive. As this extended to service organisations the profit motive was introduced into the conduct of relationships. If marriage itself was to be regulated by considerations of profit this could have disastrous consequences.

The discussion was concluded by an observation about centres of excellence and the precarious state many of them are in. A connection was made between the notion of professionalism and the capacity to safeguard resources. A firm professional base, and appropriate links between kindred practitioners, safeguarded services not only for the practioners but also, and most crucially, for their clients.

List of guests

Dr Dick Bird   *Dean of Postgraduate Training, Tavistock Clinic*
Dr Jean Packman   *Senior Lecturer, Dept of Sociology, Exeter*
Mrs Frances Love   *Director, Scottish Marriage Guidance Council*
Mrs Virginia Bottomley   *Member of Parliament*
Mr Paul Upson   *Chairman, Adolescent Dept, Tavistock Clinic*
Mr Bob Morley   *Director, Family Welfare Association*
Dr Ann Fingret   *Chief Medical Officer, BBC*
Miss Alison Webster   *Board of Social Responsibility, Church House*
Miss Shirley Goodwin   *General Secretary, Health Visitors' Association*
Mr Barry Curnow   *Chairman & Chief Exec, MSL Group International*

Listed are those who accepted an invitation to the meeting; not all were able to be present on the day.

Mr Roy Taylor *formerly Chief of Probation Inspectorate, Home Office*
Lady Jane Lloyd *Member, Institute of Family Therapy*
Dr Douglas Haldane *Psychotherapist and Consultant*
The Rt. Rev. Hugh Montefiore *formerly Bishop of Birmingham*
Mr Richard Redman *Director of Services, Relate*
The Rt. Rev. John Denis *Bishop of Ipswich*
Mrs Pat Coussell *Marital Psychotherapist, Associate staff, TIMS*
Dr John Birtchnell *Social Psychiatry Unit, Maudsley Hospital*
Mrs Eileen McCabe *Director of Counselling and Training, Catholic Marriage Advisory Council*
Rev. Peter Chambers *Marriage Education Committee, House of Bishops*
The Rt Rev. Simon Phipps *formerly Bishop of Lincoln*
Mrs Mary Welch *Analyst, former staff, TIMS*
Dr John Bowlby *Honorary Consultant Psychiatrist, Tavistock Clinic*
Mr Donald Maclean *Role Management Ltd*
Mr Tony Wells *Regional Staff Development Officer, Probation Service*
Miss Janet Mattinson *Analyst, Consultant, TIMS*
Dr Jack Dominian *Director, Marriage Research Centre*
Miss Sheila Poupard *Assistant Director, Wandsworth Social Services Department*
Miss Margery Taylor *Chairman, Family Welfare Association*
Mrs Jane Simpson *Solicitors Family Law Association*
Mrs Jean Judge *Director, Catholic Marriage Advisory Council*
Dr Martin Richards *Child Care & Development Group, Cambridge*
Mr Hugh Jenkins *Institute of Family Therapy*
Ms Pat Murray *National Children's Home*
Capt Tony Oglesby *Soldiers', Sailors' and Airmen's Families Association*
Miss Jean Hutton *Grubb Institute*

LIST OF GUESTS

Mr Ken Corcoran *Assistant Chief Inspector, Social Services, DHSS*
Mrs Bridget Hester *Tutor Consultant, Relate*
Dr Judith Trowell *Chairman, Child & Family Dept, Tavistock Clinic*
The Baroness Faithfull
Dr Michael Pokorny *Lincoln Clinic*
Mr Paul *NSPCC*
Mr Mannie Sher *Paddington Centre for Psychotherapy*
Rev. Brian Duckworth *Methodist Board of Social Responsibility*
Mr Douglas Woodhouse *Marital Psychotherapist, Associate staff, TIMS*
Ms Jean Scarlett *London Centre for Psychotherapy*
Mr Barry Estlea *Assistant Chief Probation Officer*
Mrs Ruth Schmidt *Director, Exploring Parenthood*
Mr Chris Goulding *National Training Adviser, National Children's Home*
Mrs Pamela Clulow
Mrs Lisa Parkinson *Training Officer, National Family Conciliation Council*
Mr Norman Davies *Probation Officer*
Mrs Elizabeth Bishop *Tutor Consultant, Relate*
Mr Arch Mantle *Home Office*
Professor Noel Timms *University of Leicester*
Professor Robert Shaw *Royal Free Hospital*
Mr Peter Fry *Central Council for Education and Training in Social Work*
Mr David French *Director, Relate*
Miss Una McCluskey *Department of Social Policy, University of York*
Mr Colin Thomas *Home Office Probation Inspectorate*
Ms Elizabeth Bargh *The Industrial Society*
Dr Austin Heady *Department of Clinical Epidemiology, Royal Free Hospital*
Ms Karen Lyons *North-east London Polytechnic*
Ms Christine Garrety *Bucks College of Higher Education*
Mr Phillip Hodson *LBC*
Mrs Penny de Haas *Director, Ealing Psychotherapy Centre*

Dr Arthur Hyatt-Williams   *Consultant Psychiatrist, Tavistock Clinic*
Mrs Elizabeth Hodder   *Director, Stepfamily Association*
Mr Bill Bayley   *Regional Staff Development Officer, Probation Service*
Miss Ann Shearer   *Journalist, The Guardian*
Ms Florence Rossetti   *University of Bath*
Mrs Margaret Walker   *Librarian, Tavistock Clinic*
Mr John Jones   *Divorce Court Welfare Officer, Oxford Probation Service*
Dr Michael Reddy   *ICAS*
Mr Jeffery Blumenfeld   *Director, Jewish Marriage Council*
Mrs Yvette Walczak, North London Polytechnic
Mr Paul Brown   *Journal of Sexual and Marital Therapy*
The Rev. Derek Blows   *Director, Westminster Pastoral Foundation*
Mrs Thelma Fisher   *Chairman, National Family Conciliation Council*
Mrs Renate Olins   *Relate*
Mr Maurice Caplan   *Administrator, Tavistock Clinic*
Miss Clemency Chapman   *Marital Psychotherapist, former staff, TIMS*
Mr Bill Utting   *Chief Inspector, Social Services, DHSS*
Mr Peter Needham   *Executive Management Ltd*
Mrs Susan Needham   *Relate*
Ms Bridget Ramsay   *Consultant, Organisation and Management*
Ms E C Maxwell   *English Nursing Board*
Mr Richard Lane
Mr M A Armstrong   *The Probation Service*
Mr R M Lewis   *The Probation Service*
Ms Olya Khaleelee   *London Centre for Psychotherapy*
Miss Judith Brearley   *Chairman, Scottish Marriage Guidance Council*
Mr John Schlapobersky   *Tutor Consultant, Relate*
Mrs Moira Fryer   *Head of Counselling, Relate*
Mr Ken Smith   *Group for the Advancement of Psychotherapy in Social Work*

LIST OF GUESTS

Mrs Molly Paul *formerly Home Office Probation Inspectorate*
Dr Ian Sinclair *Director of Research, National Institute for Social Work*
Mr Mike Foster *Tavistock Institute of Human Relations*
Dr Klaus Fink *Halliwick Hospital*
Mr Liam Donnellan *The Probation Service*
Mrs Margaret Robinson *Member, Institute of Family Therapy*
Mrs Antonia Shooter *Tavistock Clinic*
Mrs Doris Bates *former staff, TIMS*
Mrs Penny Mansfield *Deputy Director, Marriage Research Centre*
Mrs Beatrice Stevens *Psychotherapy Unit, Maudsley Hospital*
Mr John Cleese *Writer, actor*
Mrs Judith Stephens *Psychotherapist, former staff, TIMS*
Mrs Kathleen Bannister *former staff, TIMS*
Ms Nicola Hilliard *National Children's Bureau*
Mr Robin Blandford *Chairman, Stepfamily Association*
Mr Jafar Kareem *NAFSIYAT, Intercultural Therapy Centre*
Ms Carolyn Douglas *Director, Exploring Parenthood*
Ms Sue Slipman *National Council for One Parent Families*
Mr Robert Chester *Director of Research, Marriage Research Centre, University of Hull*
Mr M Tuck *Home Office Research and Planning Unit*
Mr David Sturgeon *University College Hospital*
Ms Ros Draper *Tavistock Clinic*
Mr Peter Linthwaite *Director of Research, Health Education Authority*
Ms Jane Lovell *Inner London Education Authority*
Mr Nick Tyndall *Training Officer, CRUSE*
Ms Gill Brown *Smith Bundy Video*
Dr Shanti Ponnappa *Psychiatrist and Psychotherapist*
Dr Judith Barnard *General Practitioner and Psychotherapist*

Mrs Joan Reggiori   *Psychotherapist*
Mrs Joan Hall   *former staff, TIMS*
Ms Sheila Ernst   *Women's Therapy Centre*
Mr Tim Dartington   *National Council for Voluntary Organisations*
Ms Jenny Hope   *Journalist, 'Daily Mail'*
Ms Pamela Mann   *Woodberry Down Child Guidance Clinic*
Mr Geoffrey Parkinson   *The Probation Service*
Ms Alexandra Fanning   *Arbours Association*
Mrs Jessica Skippon   *Skippon Video Associates*
Mr Peter Hildebrand   *Tavistock Clinic*
Ms Denise Mumford   *Wandsworth Social Services Dept*
Mr Eric Miller   *Tavistock Institute of Human Relations*
Ms Alix Kirsta   *Freelance journalist*
Mrs Sasha Brooks   *Trainee, TIMS*
Mrs Gina Allen   *former staff, TIMS*
Mrs Helen Tarsh   *Trainee, TIMS*
Ms Jo Rosenthall   *Trainee, TIMS*
Mrs Pauline Hodson   *Trainee, TIMS*
Ms Helen Franks   *Freelance journalist*
Dr Mark Aveline   *Psychiatrist, Mapperley Hospital*
Dr Jack Waldman   *Psychiatrist, Haringey Child Guidance Centre*
Miss Jenny Beddington   *Social Worker, Royal Free Hospital*
Mrs Lynne Cudmore   *Staff, TIMS*
Mrs Elaine Bollinghaus   *Trainee, TIMS*
Ms Viv Taylor Gee   *Thames TV*
Dr Joan Lewis   *London School of Economics*
Dr M Wieselberg   *Middlesex Hospital*
Ms Barbara Lantin   *Journalist, 'The Jewish Chronicle'*
Mr John Deith   *Royal Association in Aid of the Deaf and Dumb*
Mrs Margaret Inglis   *Royal Free Hospital*
Mrs Gerlind Richards   *Secretary, International Union of Family Organisations*
Mr William Richards   *Sun Life Investment Management*

Dr B Rudd   *General Practitioner*
Professor the Rev. Canon Gordon Dunstan   *Chairman, Tavistock Institute of Medical Psychology*
Mr Timothy Renton   *Member of Parliament, Minister of State, Home Office*
Mr David Clark   *Research Fellow, City of Sheffield Polytechnic*
Dr Robin Skynner   *former Chairman, Institute of Family Therapy*
Mrs Betty Simpson   *Secretary Tavistock Institute of Medical Psychology*
Mrs Elspeth Morley   *Psychotherapist*
Dr I Fairbairn   *Psychiatrist, Edgware General Hospital*
Mrs Joan Maizels   *Psychologist*
Dr Oscar Hill   *Psychiatrist, Middlesex Hospital*
Mrs Elma Sinclair
Mr George Hume   *Secretary and Finance Officer, Tavistock Institute of Medical Psychology*
Miss Jane Newton   *former staff, TIMS*
Ms Julia Orange   *Journalist*
Miss Lynette Hughes   *Staff, TIMS*
Miss Felicia Olney   *Staff, TIMS*
Ms Joanna Foster   *Chair, Equal Opportunities Commission*
Mrs Pat Hunt   *Tutor Consultant, Relate*
Mr Trevor Jaggar   *General Manager, Social Responsibility and Education, Quakers*
Mr Trevor Berry   *Families Need Fathers*
Mrs Rani Atma   *Asian Family Counselling Service*
The Baroness Seear
Dr David Owens   *Director, National Association for the Childless*
Mr Don Bryant   *Tavistock Institute of Human Relations*
Mrs Enid Balint   *Psychoanalyst, Consultant, TIMS*
Ms Anne Spackman   *Journalist, 'The Independent'*
Ms Carolyn Okell-Jones   *Tavistock Clinic*
Mr Robert Young   *Editor, Free Associations Books*
Dr Sebastian Kraemer   *Tavistock Clinic*

Ms Barbara Jones *Journalist, 'Mail on Sunday'*
Mr Christopher Clulow *Chairman, TIMS*
Mr Stan Ruszczynski *Deputy Chairman, TIMS*
Mr Fred Balfour *Associate Staff, TIMS*
Miss Linda Binnington *Staff, TIMS*
Miss Evelyn Cleavely *Staff, TIMS*
Mrs Nina Cohen *Staff, TIMS*
Mr Warren Colman *Staff, TIMS*
Miss Diana Daniell *Staff, TIMS*
Mrs Barbara Dearnley *Staff, TIMS*
Mrs Benita Dyal *Staff, TIMS*
Mr Peter Fullerton *Staff, TIMS*
Mrs Laura Kreitman *Staff, TIMS*
Dr Malcolm Millington *Consultant, TIMS*
Mr Paul Pengelly *Staff, TIMS*
Miss Margaret Spooner *Staff, TIMS*
Mr Christopher Vincent *Staff, TIMS*

PART TWO

The Tavistock Institute of Marital Studies: evolution of a marital agency

Douglas Woodhouse

Introduction

John Muir, the naturalist, is credited with saying, 'When we try to pick out anything by itself, we usually find it hitched to everything else in the universe'. Only some of the salient linkages in the evolution of the Tavistock Institute of Marital Studies can be identified here—and other writers would be likely to construe the pattern differently. Then, of course, there is serendipity and that crucial chemistry emerging from the interplay, at any given time, of particular people with their distinctive attributes and their destructive as well as creative impulses. Their influence is only implied in what follows though they were, of course, crucial in shaping the TIMS and the events discussed.

The account deals with the evolution of a non-medical therapeutic unit concerned with interactive processes and their understanding in the light of work with couples experiencing difficulty in their relationship. It is therefore concerned with intra- and inter-personal conflict and its function in the individual's quest for personal development, and with marriage as a paradigm for impediments to relatedness in some other human systems.

J. D. Sutherland's *The Psychodynamic Image of Man* and his concept of 'care' (Sutherland, 1980) best convey the philosophy of the TIMS, one it has shared with others in the Tavistock matrix within which the unit was nurtured and its adaptive capacities were fostered. Significant phases in the organisation's development are identified in the first part of the paper. It is referred to by the name it bore at the time of the events discussed, Family Discussion Bureau, until 1968, the Institute of Marital Studies until 1988, and thereafter the Tavistock Institute of Marital Studies. The second part of this book is concerned with the main thrust of conceptual development over the forty years since the unit's inception.

Historical development

The beginning:
The Family Discussion Bureau

Events leading to the establishment of the Family Discussion Bureau in 1948 were part of processes set in train by the Second World War. The social and political climate fostered by the war stimulated a quest for a more equitable society, and a more humane as well as a more effective response to those in need. An implicit assumption of an ordered, stable and highly stratified society where material and rational needs and motives, based on a generally accepted set of values, were predominant in determining the behaviour of human beings was giving way to an acknowledgement of the part played by immaterial, irrational psychological factors in human problems and their solution. The limitations of material help, advice and precept alone in achieving these ends were increasingly apparent (Wilson, 1951).

Extensive health and welfare legislation associated with the shift in values had a profound impact on social work, from which the unit grew. An influential report on the employment and training of social workers, for example, noted that though their clients had been and were largely still to be found among the poor, this was likely to be less exclusively so in future. The reappraisal called for was one that included attention to the interaction of the inner and outer world of those in difficulty (Younghusband, 1947).

Marital stress at the end of the war

Citizens Advice Bureaux were set up as part of the preparation for war. With the peace, they became concerned with problems resulting from social dislocation and with the many questions raised by the new social legislation. The director of the Bureaux in London[1] recognised the leading part played by marital problems and related family stress in the ostensibly practical difficulties of the people served. At the same time, concern about the rising incidence of divorce, principally of those in marriages contracted during the war, prompted two official enquiries. The first advocated a marriage welfare service, sponsored but not run by the state, the second made recommendations that eventually led to financial support from central government to approved agencies offering help to people experiencing marital difficulties.[2] Experiment and gradual evolution was encouraged in this still uncharted field. The social trends were congruent, favouring investigation of the phenomena of marital conflict and stress, of the problems of access to those experiencing it and of making an effective response.

A collaborative pilot experiment

CABs in London had been administered by the Family Welfare Association (FWA). Founded in 1869 as the Charity Organisation Society, it changed its name in 1946 on account of the great extension of statutory social services and in order to stress its primary aim: the promotion of family well-being by the methods of social casework. This was the oldest social work organisation in the country, with a long tradition of advocacy for social reform and experimentation, one which was playing an important part in establishing professional training for social workers. But the organisation inevitably embodied aspects of pre-war social theory and attitudes alongside the impetus to innovation.

CAB experience was reinforced by that of FWA social workers who were increasingly presented with marital and family problems that defeated them. On the basis of her growing conviction that disturbed personal relationships lay behind many of the problems presented to social agencies, the war-time CAB director initiated the formation of a small group of FWA staff in 1948 to explore the possibility of offering more effective help. Mobilizing the group led to the conviction that technical support had to be found from outside their own organisation and beyond contemporary social casework. It was from the Tavistock Clinic and the Tavistock Institute of Human Relations, with their psychoanalytic and socio-dynamic orientations, that help was sought with staff training and the problems of organisational and strategic development.[3] No issue of principle was raised; in 1945 the 'Tavistock group' that formed after the war had designated marriage and marital stress as one of an array of concerns comprising an integrate within the medical and social fields to which it should address itself (Dicks, 1970). Professional consultancy was established very soon after the pilot experiment was authorized and sufficiently funded, involving staff of both Clinic and Institute.[4] Thus, collaboration began with the experimental group in the role of 'client organisation'.

Consultation and collaboration

There was sufficient agreement on the part of the new group and other relevant members of the FWA with the tenets guiding the approach of the Tavistock to make collaboration possible and for members of the TIHR to participate in the work of the steering committee set up to guide the new endeavour (Wilson et al., 1949a). Among them, the following were salient:

1. The need to link training and research with casework, so as to close the gap between theory and practice and provide opportunity for the formulation and testing of working hypotheses. The three activities needed to be kept in balance for the enterprise to be technically viable.
2. That the human problems with which the group was concerned could only be studied at the necessary depth by making use of therapeutic situations—the client/worker relationship.
3. That understanding required an opportunity to combine reflection with skill derived from practical efforts to diagnose and treat the 'real life' problems of clients.
4. An endorsement of the casework principle that nothing effective can be done to or for people, only *with* them. [Wilson, 1947a, 1947b, 1949b]

A set of activities was pursued during the initial five years, the time originally allotted to the pilot experiment. First, and before casework began, what amounted to consumer research was undertaken in two areas of London to discover needs and acceptable approaches to marital and family relationship problems.

Group discussions with a wide range of people who had not openly sought help confirmed the need for a new service. Severe problems evidently existed within the healthy part of the community; the line between so-called normal families who could cope and those threatened by crisis proved difficult if not impossible to draw. At that time, stigma was attached to marital difficulty. Few people, then, were able to ask for help with their relationships before difficulties became acute and disturbing, but, with that point reached, it was acceptable if made available in a way that did not imply social failure. Even so it became clear that the majority of clients would be referred by workers in community service.

These open discussions led to the title 'Family Discussion Bureaux' in place of 'Marriage Welfare'. 'Family discussion' was neutral, applicable alike to preventive and therapeutic work, and suggested the joint, client/worker nature of the task (Menzies, 1949; Bannister et al., 1955).

The second task was to explore the possibility of using psychoanalytic theory of personality in the development of a casework approach to marital problems. Those seeking help with such problems seldom regarded them as a medical matter nor themselves as psychiatric patients, but some of the special knowledge of the psychoanalytically trained psychiatrist was necessary for those wishing to give effective help to people with problems stemming from motives of which they were unaware. Making such knowledge available raised big issues for the analysts, but their doubts were met by the forceful argument that troubled marriages existed and, because the dis-ease was not medical, were not getting the psychological help they needed. Meanwhile, the Tavistock doctors concerned had a special interest in exploring the implications of extending caseworkers' skills.

The basic task of the FDB group was to gain such understanding of themselves as would keep them free from the emotional pressure exerted by clients and permit them to see the conflicting forces at work with sufficient detachment to get a clear picture of them (Sutherland, 1955) and they had to learn to reflect on and evaluate their own subjective experience; '. . . a limited though considerable change in personality was necessary for the new skill, though the amount of change necessary could only be judged as the work progressed' (Balint, quoted by Sutherland, 1955; see also Balint, 1954; 1964).

The focus that then developed was not so much on the psychodynamics of the individual as on the marital relationship—the process of interaction between the psychodynamic features of the two individuals concerned. The marital relationship was conceived in systemic terms from the start as was the family of which this relationship is the nucleus.

The container within which reflection was combined with the practical experience of treating real problems was the weekly case conference. Learning took place through the medium of the relationship developed between consultant analyst and the group of caseworkers and between member and member (Bannister et al., 1955).

The third separate, but complementary, component of these initial explorations was an investigation of patterns of living in ordinary urban families, an attempt to understand their social and psychological organisation. A social anthropologist and a social psychologist had major responsibility for the work in collaboration with FDB consultants, some of its caseworkers and psychologists from the Tavistock Clinic. This research was jointly sponsored by the TIHR and the FWA (Bott, 1957). Besides the value of the interpretations and hypotheses developed because of what they added to concepts emerging from the casework—the study was of marriage as much as of families—it enriched the texture of interdisciplinary collaboration in the group as a whole.

The move to the Tavistock

The staff had consolidated as a working group and were established in one location when the time allotted to the pilot project expired. The question of continuing the unit on a permanent basis became pressing and difficult; the difficulties were two-fold and reinforced one another. Casework practice in the FWA, as elsewhere, was becoming more psychodynamic, but the organisation as a whole had to grapple with the task of adapting to post-war conditions and values. The changes demanded were considerable and, given the legacy of its history, far from easy for the FWA. For the FDB, meanwhile, preoccupation with the development of professional competence in its specialized field and close involvement with Tavistock personnel militated against its integration into the professional life and culture of its parent organisation. Neither the task nor the sentient boundaries of the FDB now coincided sufficiently with those of the FWA for it to function and develop in this context (Miller & Rice, 1967). But though the FDB and its work were receiving recognition, it was not viable independently. The leadership[5] and the staff were, however, determined on its survival and were supported in this by Tavistock members of the steering committee. They undertook to explore the possibility of the unit's transfer to the TIHR; a solution was found when the FDB became one of a growing number of 'clinic linked' activities of the TIHR late in 1956 (Dicks, 1970).

Some implications of location in the Tavistock

The move strengthened the working relationship with the Tavistock Clinic at the same time as the unit's membership of TIHR underlined its non-medical status. A marital unit had existed within the Clinic, as part of the National Health Service since 1949 and was available to those referred through medical channels. With the addition of the FDB to the Tavistock's collective resources, an alternative non-medical pathway to help with marital problems now became available. The earlier exploratory work made clear that much, if not most, marital difficulty and stress presented itself indirectly, particularly in the first instance through 'social symptoms' to a variety of practitioners in a range of different agencies. The pilot experiment also confirmed the vagueness of the threshold beyond which cases could be regarded as medical problems; the wry observation of a former Tavistock colleague[6] that 'Providence had not seen fit to divide up human problems into the same categories as University Chairs' was apposite.

Once within the Tavistock, the FDB was located on the boundary between the medical and social spheres of operation and was confronted with tensions inherent in that position. To these tensions were added those emanating from its primary task with marital stress and conflict. They were technical, operational, institutional and environmental—and they were interlinked.

The technical problems were complex and remain so since they stem from developing conceptions of community mental health and differences about the understanding necessary for its promotion (Sutherland, 1971). In the case of the FDB, however, significant tension in the technical region lay in the uncertain distinction between casework and psychotherapy rooted in psychoanalysis and medical intervention. The staff were case-workers, a professional identity preserved for many years till that of 'marital therapist' was assumed in the mid-1980s. The tension referred to here is implicit in a contemporary paper by one of the Bureau's consultants.

> You will observe that personal analysis had been excluded from the training. In the Family Discussion Bureau we have deliberately held to a policy of not requiring it, and our experience has shown that good work can be done without. Whether or not the work is better without it, it would be impossible to say. Certainly some of those caseworkers who have not been analysed previously do not wish to take this training now, as they feel they might then want to become more like the analyst. On the other hand, those who have had some personal analysis find that they can work easily at the same 'levels' and in the same way as other caseworkers. [Sutherland, 1956]

Operational tensions were related to, but distinguishable from the technical ones. An indication of them is found in changes in the patterns of referral and the network of community services with which the FDB was thereby connected. When the transfer from the FWA to the Tavistock took place, the Bureau's clients were exclusively referred by CAB workers, social workers in various settings and probation officers. Thereafter medical referrals, notably by general practitioners, progressively replaced them and still preponderate among referred cases. Latterly, self-referred cases have attained a majority,[7] but 'hidden referrers' are often implicated in such applications and many of these are doctors. Thus, operational connectedness shifted towards the medical network and, while the unit's experience has been that the distinction between the 'social' and 'medical' in this field is unhelpful, some sociologists and social theorists remain critical of what has been called the 'medicalisation of marriage' (Morgan, 1985).

Institutional tensions were inherent in a situation in which working relationships with the National Health Service Clinic preponderated over those with the independent Institute of Human Relations which carried legal, administrative and financial responsibility for the unit. In this respect the FDB was in the same position as other 'clinic-linked' units. However, these had been generated within the organisation whereas the Bureau had been introduced into it from outside; an important factor in the negotiations leading to its transfer from the FWA had been the judgement that with support from central and local government, it would become self-financing. This was (and has continued to be) a difficult position to achieve. On numerous occasions survival was only secured through the willingness of the TIHR to underwrite prospective deficits, thus affording a breathing space in which to reach solvency. A strategy to meet the problem was seriously debated soon after the FDB became part of the Tavistock—to work towards the transfer of its staff to the Clinic as and when the NHS establishment increased. A small number of staff holding Clinic posts were seconded for work in the FDB for some years, but the strategy was abandoned as an ultimate solution, the prospect of financial uncertainty and constraint being accepted in order to maintain a position outside the medical domain.

In addition there are influences from the wider environment. Associated with effects on the Bureau of government grants-in-aid of its work, which are permissive not mandatory and are subject to the ebb and flow of the economic climate and political opinion, are less tangible ones arising from conflicts of feeling related to the highly personal, primary relationship of marriage. The community's concern about the social and mental health implications of marriage breakdown and stress is, in part, reflected through official funding. However, the paradoxical nature of marriage as a personal relationship and as a social institution, within which there is both freedom and constraint (Lyons, 1973), makes for ambivalence at governmental, organisational and personal levels. Notwithstanding changed attitudes and increasing openness since the unit was founded, support for intensive study and therapeutic intervention in this field remains equivocal.

Some of these problems followed from and all were highlighted by the move from the FWA. Their containment or resolution within the Tavistock has done much to shape the unit, its character and current identity.

Developments within the Tavistock: practice, training and research

The concept of the practice, training and research 'mix' as a total function was implicit in the pilot experiment. The FDB project itself represented such an amalgam, practice being the vehicle for staff training and the enterprise as a whole a research endeavour. But the idea began to be applied as an operational strategy following transfer to the Tavistock, a development accelerated when the TIHR acquired additional premises and the Bureau was able to move into the same building as the Clinic (Dicks, 1970). The interdependence of the three activities is of the essence, each informing and being informed by the other to sustain professional growth and external relevance. However, the core activity is work with disturbed marriages; practice is therefore considered first.

Practice and the service component

Demands for help led other organisations in this field to multiply the number of centres providing it. This was the model embodied in the pilot work and the establishment of two FDB offices. Dual location was given up for practical reasons; in any case, experience pointed to the need for an alternative approach. Specialist services were indeed called for, but most marital and related family problems present themselves indirectly: 'people knock on many different doors' as a government working party studying marital problems and the helping services noted later (Home Office, 1979). Practitioners in community services are 'front line' professionals in a position to recognise such problems in their early stages and to respond in ways appropriate to their patients' or clients' perceptions and to their particular tasks and roles. If they can do so, the aims of prevention and of economy in the use of scarce specialist resources may be met simultaneously—given, that is, that the practitioners concerned have the requisite understanding and skill.

This appraisal suggested an alternative approach to prevention from the educational one originally envisaged for the FDB—through pre-marriage counselling, work in schools and youth clubs, for example (Bannister et al., 1955). However, a comprehensive service calls for the provision of training opportunities for relevant practitioners at professional and post-graduate levels and the technical support of the specialists. The effectiveness and credibility of such training requires diversity of competence on the part of the trainers. They need themselves to practice at an advanced level, to communicate straightforwardly the theoretical principles on which their work is based and to collaborate with non-specialists in their application (see also Sutherland, 1967, 1968, regarding the psychotherapist's role in community services).

In the years immediately following the move to the Tavistock, energies were mainly devoted to staff development through the provision of service and to a fuller exposition of the Bureau's work than had hitherto been possible. *Marriage: studies in emotional conflict and growth* (Pincus, 1960) described practice with a range of troubled marriages. It took account of unconscious processes that influence an individual's choice of partner and discussed the nature of and psychic purposes that can lie behind conflict in the interaction between couples. As the title of the book suggests, the work emphasised the benign as well as the destructive aspects of conflict for personal development and maturation in marriage.

FDB staff were not, of course, the first or the only ones to base their understanding of marital problems and interaction on the psychoanalytic theory of personality development. It was the function of the working-group and the four-person therapeutic relationship, the technique by then established, that could claim to be unique.[8]

Theoretical developments are discussed in the second part of this paper, but it should be noted here that the employment of a 'therapeutic pair' with couples developed out of the pilot experiment. Because the possibilities of creative change in the marital relationship had been generally found to be greater when both partners were involved, the Bureau had come to work exclusively with couples. However, the involvement of one caseworker with two clients so added to the complexities of transference and countertransference that two workers were soon deployed to avoid them. It had also been realized that the technique had a potential for staff training, the less experienced learning from work and discussion with more experienced colleagues (Bannister et al., 1955). Later, however, it was observed that the relationship developed between the caseworkers in any given case tended to mirror important aspects of the client–couple's interaction. That is, the therapeutic relationship system was influenced by that of the clients. Scrutiny of this unconsciously determined phenomena, so that caseworkers became consciously aware of it, could advance understanding of the couple's difficulties and make such insights accessible in the work. Some characteristics of the weekly case-conference where such scrutiny routinely takes place have changed over time as the staff group has become more sophisticated and those with and without analytic experience and training more evenly balanced, so that the role of the psychiatrist/psychoanalyst has become less prominent. The distinctive influence of the case-conference on the unit remains, however, and is conveyed by the following:

> It is clear that in order to keep their vital self-awareness and to understand as far as possible, the extent to which their own involvement may be distorting their understanding of their clients' difficulties, the caseworkers need a medium in which they, too, may develop and feel free to involve themselves in relationships. Without such freedom it would become very difficult for them to avoid working in mental blinkers which would prevent them from seeing anything except the rational content of their clients' complaints and fears, and of their own anxieties. The group provides a setting in which these anxieties can be aired and tolerated. Caseworkers have an opportunity to discuss their cases in conference, but the constant gain in casework experience which this provides is seen as incidental to the vital atmosphere created by the group which can be internalized so that workers carry it with them to their clients. It is essential that the atmosphere should be predominantly accepting and supportive so that the workers can be spontaneous in their discussions, knowing as they do that these will reveal hidden aspects of their own personalities. But, in so far as the group avoids a destructively critical attitude, it must, nevertheless, make demands on its members, the chief being for a disciplined and discriminating attitude to their work. [Pincus, 1960]

The training component

Alongside the continuing emphasis on staff development, the training of allied professionals began immediately following the Bureau's transfer to the Tavistock as a result of a request for a training course for probation officers. This occurred at a time when their matrimonial casework service in magistrates' courts was growing. While policy changes have progressively diminished their civil court work, the implications of stress in marital and family relationships for work with offenders became increasingly apparent. The courses developed into an annual event, sponsored by central government (the Probation and Aftercare Department of the Home Office), and continued without a break for thirty years.

The longevity of these events, though significant, was not their most important feature. This lay in their function as a 'laboratory' in which to develop concepts, test patterns of training courses and apply the experience acquired from practice within the unit, especially the role of the working-group in learning.

The term 'working-group' in this context has particular connotations. It is no accident that practitioners concerned with marital work, and therefore with manifestations of intra-psychic processes in inter-personal relationships, should find themselves paying attention to the group as a vehicle for containing and working-through the emotional impact of learning and working in this field. They could not be unaware, in themselves as in their clients, of resistance to personal change. From war-time experience and later of group therapy in the Tavistock Clinic, Bion (1961) observed and documented processes by which members of a group can unconsciously co-operate in avoiding the struggle with its real task. The parallel with ways in which couples can unconsciously co-operate to maintain illusions about themselves and each other is striking. Alongside the impetus for change and development goes what Bion described as a hatred of learning about the self and of the experience of uncertainty which this invariably entails—until the individual gains some mastery and is able to assume that degree of personal autonomy and manifest concern required for reality-based co-operation with others.

Bion's work in the Clinic had a profound influence within the Tavistock as a whole and stimulated collaboration between the Clinic and the TIHR in what came to be known as group relations training (Trist and Sofer, 1959; Rice, 1965). The evolving structure and content of FDB courses drew on this growing body of experience to facilitate the assimilation of new learning into professional skill. This, while it affords freedom, also imposes additional responsibility, a burden which, with parts of himself, the practitioner seeks to be rescued (Woodhouse, 1967a). Meanwhile, FDB staff became progressively more involved with group relations conferences as part of their own 'in-house' training and as members of conference staff.

The work with probation officers was a precursor to a wide range of extra-mural courses and training events involving allied practitioners and their employing institutions in the statutory and voluntary services (e.g. Marriage Guidance Councils) in addition to universities and training organisations in the United Kingdom and abroad (E. Balint, 1959; Bannister and Pincus, 1966; Woodhouse, 1967b, 1970).

The beginning of intra-mural training was also linked to work with the probation service following an approach to the Tavistock Clinic by the Home Office. In the year following the first extra-mural course, the first experienced probation officers were seconded for supervised marital casework in the unit. They, and the officers who followed, became in-service tutors to colleagues undertaking marital work in the courts.

In the decade that followed its establishment within the Tavistock, the FDB received Foundation support specifically for the provision of fellowships for United Kingdom and overseas post-graduate students. These were practitioners and practitioner-teachers, principally from probation and social work and, increasingly, the Marriage Guidance movement in the U.K., as well as medical and social workers from abroad, who would return to key roles in their employing organisations. It became policy to 'train the trainers', a corollary being the extension of supervisory skills related to practice outside the specialized setting of the FDB.

The growing volume of training within and beyond the unit stimulated collaboration with others in the Tavistock concerned with inter-disciplinary teaching, primarily through the clinic-linked School of Family Psychiatry and Community Mental Health. An important aspect of training is that it enables direct contact to be maintained with the preoccupations and working problems of those in the field and with developments abroad. Training also becomes an important source of recruitment when internal students or those invited onto the staff of training events apply and are selected to join the unit. Their experience in other settings enriches its knowledge-base and, through them, links with community services are strengthened.

Research and publication

Following the appearance of *Marriage: Studies in Emotional Conflict and Growth* (Pincus, 1960), stimulus for research and publications came from three related sources: increasingly varied experience of training and consultancy; participation in conferences and symposia at home and overseas, and, as a foundation to both, work with couples seen in the unit. Alongside the publication of journal articles, a monograph series was established under the unit's imprint to make less than book-length material available, particularly to students.

Burgeoning demands on the unit for help with training led to a national conference organized by the FDB for a multi-disciplinary group of trainers and social work teachers. Papers by staff and former students from the probation and community mental health services, together with discussion of the timing and method of teaching about marital interaction and their impact on students, were included in a widely read monograph (Institute of Marital Studies, 1962).

The study and comparison of cases seen in the unit which showed the operation of phantasies shared by couples at different levels of personality development, and distinguished different levels of unconscious defences against anxiety, led to better understanding of the four-person relationship and, through differential use of conjoint ('foursome') and individual sessions, to the enhancement of the therapeutic process (Bannister and Pincus, 1965; Lyons, 1973). A parallel study enabled the case to be argued for brief intensive work in a context that helped practitioners withstand the pressures exerted by disturbed clients in crisis (Guthrie and Mattinson, 1971).

A trend then began, one that accelerated thereafter, in which wider applications were made of experience and theory derived from practice within the unit and from training and consultancy outside it. For example, evidence was submitted jointly with the Clinic's marital unit to a government-appointed committee set up in 1965 to consider the changes necessary to secure effective local authority personal and family services.[9] At the same time, reform of the law of divorce was under debate and the unit contributed to a Memorandum to it. These were the basis for an outline strategy to promote comprehensive services for the family, preventive as well as remedial, taking account of the interdependence of the mental health aspects of marriage and divorce, the impact of social change and the requirements of professional training, practice and co-operation (Woodhouse, 1969).

Meanwhile, unconscious processes manifest in the interaction within and between relationship systems were a continuing preoccupation and were explored in a number of different areas. For example, there was work in the field of mental handicap. This examined the marital participation and interaction of couples previously resident in a hospital for the subnormal, in an attempt to understand why many subjects considered handicapped when single had been able to use the commitment to their partners for their own personal development (Mattinson, 1970). Other work, arising from consultancy in a children's hospital, was based on treatment of couples having a child suffering from recalcitrant illnesses (encopresis and asthma). This led to efforts to develop an approach to understanding and helping such sick children through working with the marital interaction of their parents (Mainprice, 1974). A third area of exploration derived from long-term collaboration with university teachers of social work students and their fieldwork supervisors (Mattinson, 1975) and is discussed further in the second part of this paper.

The Institute of Marital Studies: autonomy within the Tavistock

The Clinic and Institute of Human Relations had been growing apace in terms of the range of their activities and, particularly the latter, in terms of the number of staff involved. Institute units and some Clinic activities had become progressively dispersed around a number of sites, militating against the interchange and close relationships necessary to sustain coherence. The situation had long been foreseen and equally long negotiations with the relevant organs of the Health Service at last resulted in purpose-built accommodation to house both organisations. When this opened, it was possible for the Clinic and almost the entire Institute to be under one roof again. Meanwhile, expansion and diversification of operational interests required reorganisation of the Institute's management structure.

By this time the FDB had developed into an advanced centre in its field, and it achieved autonomy as part of these organisational changes. In place of the status of 'clinic-linked unit', it became self-managing and, along with the other working-groups, assumed responsibility for the corporate management of the TIHR under the authority of its Council and moved with them into the new building. In 1968, the unit took the title, Institute of Marital Studies. The intention was to reflect its investment in training and research based on therapeutic practice and to convey more accurately to central government and funding bodies the nature of its work and field of enquiry in an effort to ameliorate continuing financial and related staffing problems.

Technical development, external relations and environmental change

Balint's earlier observation that a limited but still significant change in personality was required for psychodynamic understanding to find effective expression in practice had been amply confirmed by both staff and student training. From the pilot experiment of the late 1940s onwards, a model and structure for professional education had been evolving in the Tavistock to facilitate the necessary but inevitably uneven process of personal change. The working environments of IMS trainees from community services was, of course, different. Often it was far from facilitating, even in organisations that ostensibly espoused training of the kind offered. Plainly, effort and resources devoted to it—by the IMS, its trainees and their employing authorities—were vitiated insofar as the integration of newly acquired skills was impeded by as yet poorly understood problems in application and by institutional ambivalence. The efficacy of the IMS as an advanced centre within its relevant network of community services turned on a better appreciation of these issues.

By now, therapeutic work and training were making important contributions to IMS budgets; the staff, too, through the contribution of considerable unpaid time and, for example, by making over to the unit all income from writing. By contrast, such research costs as had so far been incurred had been met out of general funds. A period of rapidly rising inflation now raised financial uncertainty to an insupportable level. Technical innovations were inextricably bound up with these pressures, the more so in a small working group organized to ensure collective responsibility for its affairs. The interplay of these two concerns—problems inherent in a focus on marriage and a psychodynamic approach to marital stress in non-specialist, mainly large-scale organisations, on the one hand, and those of survival-threatening underfunding on the other—increasingly influenced operational strategy and tactics.

Negotiation of long-term training commitments which provided a continuing interface with the managers of community services became more prominent. These facilitated mutual influence at the level of the organisational system and, at the same time, eased problems of forward financial planning. Technical and financial considerations also combined to promote action-research projects and programmes supported by Trusts and Foundations.

The first such project was undertaken in a London Social Services department. Over a period of three years following a pilot phase, four staff were participant observers in the department and worked directly with a sample of clients to whom the organisation gave a high priority (Mattinson and Sinclair, 1979). The project, referred to again later, was seminal for the IMS in a number of ways. It began a process through which experience of negotiation with other institutions was widened and deepened. It established a pattern of collaborative action research which was to be influential in the unit's development. It provided direct experience of the stressful working-world of colleagues in community services. Through the staff involved, task-related anxiety was brought back into the IMS; the new work had to be accommodated emotionally as well as organisationally by the total working group, including administrative staff. The unit had to find ways in which to perform a function for projects analagous to that of the case conference for the therapeutic work. It broadened the search for relevant theory through which to explain the phenomena encountered. In addition, it gave added emphasis to the need for expansion; for a critical mass sufficient to accommodate this kind of research, the development of therapeutic work and training and to enable the IMS to respond to unpredictable events and opportunities. Again we see the interweaving of the social, the organisational/administrative and the technical aspects of the unit's multiple tasks.

Intensification of relationships between the IMS and other related organisations through training and field-based action research had parallels in the area of policy. Regular consultation between the IMS and the other major organisations in receipt of government grants-in-aid of their marital work were by now well established. Out of consideration of their different but complementary roles came a joint approach to central government seeking a national review of marital work and services in the light of knowledge and experience gained since the field had last been reviewed in the Denning Report in 1947. As a result, a multi-disciplinary working party was set up on which the IMS was represented. It published its report in the form of a consultative document, *Marriage Matters* (Home Office, 1979).

This confirmed how wide was the span of agencies and professional disciplines involved with marital difficulties in their various guises. It was found that, though not administratively conceived as such, clients/patients themselves effectively defined a network of services by virtue of the needs and problems they presented. These agencies and practitioners, while varied in terms of their primary tasks, had in common the need to understand the nature of marital interaction and its effect on their work. Problems of inter-professional collaboration bedeviling effectiveness, especially at field level, were emphasised. A co-ordinating role was envisaged for government with a small central unit to promote the better use of existing local resources by the development of practice and training and a strategy for research. The aim of the consultative document was to stimulate debate—as a prelude to change within government and among the many professionals and agencies that had involved themselves in the working party's activities.

However, the working party was set up by one administration, but the report was published and the consultation process launched just as another came into office; the necessary central initiative was not forthcoming. Though the professional debate began, agency managers and practitioners were soon preoccupied with the effects of restrictions on public expenditure that then ensued. The seeds of these developments, manifest following a change of government were, of course, to be found in the preceding period, one during which welfare services and the caring professions had greatly expanded.[10]

The emerging social climate revealed contradictions even more starkly than those observable hitherto. For example, there had been growing recognition that collaboration, interdependence and the interplay of differences were as requisite for the development of institutions as they were for individuals, couples and families. These values were articulated at the same time as anxiety was increasingly voiced about the finite nature of resources in the face of escalating demands. This led to defensive, reactive strategies. Such defences were always ready to be evoked, particularly in the marital field, as noted earlier. They were now fostered by the situations in which many practitioners and their managers found themselves. The external boundaries of groups and organisations tended to become less permeable as preoccupation with survival and stress among practitioners increased. Lack of resources was invoked as an irrefutable reason for limiting the time-span of commitment. Tension between autonomy and dependency was increasingly dealt with by an aggressive emphasis on independence. Reliance on techniques in treatment and training, and the avoidance of sustained relationships, grew; a premium came to be put on short-term remedies for the ills of a growing number and range of 'casualties'. Reductionist attitudes rather than those encouraging attention to process and the interplay of the inner and outer world of those in difficulty were reinforced. As Sutherland (1980) pointed out, 'the pluralism in approaches thus reflects a situation not so much as stimulating differences within a healthy enterprise as one with serious and dangerous contradictions'.

Re-drawing Tavistock boundaries

Trends within and external forces bearing on the Tavistock Clinic and the Tavistock Institute of Human Relations up to the time the IMS became an autonomous unit within the TIHR have been recorded by Dicks (1970) and by Gray (1970). Thereafter, the developing social and political trends and contradictions inevitably influenced both organisations. The Tavistock Clinic was faced with the need to preserve its psychoanalytically based activities and its international status within a restricted and restrictive National Health Service. The TIHR, too, felt their impact; the total staff-group declined in size as the pattern and volume of public and private sector social science research altered and contracted; differentiation of the spheres of activity and interest of the various units became more marked. So did those of the Clinic and Institute.

The changing focus and practice of the major part of the TIHR also became less congruent with those of the IMS and, in 1979, the unit transferred to the Tavistock Institute of Medical Psychology. This charitable foundation, the founding body, first of the Clinic and then of the TIHR, having retained a supportive role in relation to both organisations, assumed legal responsibility for the IMS. The new arrangement aimed to leave the unit free to maintain its working relationship with the Clinic and relevant activities of the Institute (e.g. its group relations training work) and to adopt a distinctive form or organisation more suited to its future adaptive needs.

Continuity in change

The preceding statement of a fundamental change does scant justice to the actual experience of it. While in train, it was often difficult to distinguish whether the process was one of destructive fission or creative potential leading to the re-drawing of boundaries in the interests of mutual development. The conflict and tension inherent in this institutional change were familiar to IMS staff from day-to-day work with couples struggling to find a more effective and satisfying distance from each other. The culture of the unit, a product of collective experience of therapeutic work, in which loss and change are persistent themes, helped to sustain the working group through the transition.

In its new context, the unit engaged in a series of collaborative and substantially funded enterprises following on from the Social Services department project. One such grew out of therapy with marital stress precipitated by the advent of a child, often the first-born. With groups of health visitors, this project sought to develop a preventive model by which to enhance the capacity of couples to contain the tension inherent in the transition from two to three. It questioned the proposition of 'crisis theorists' that pregnancy is a propitious time for prophylactic mental health intervention (Clulow, 1982). Other work involved participation in a programme set up within the Probation Service aimed at effecting settlements between divorcing couples subject to welfare enquiries to protect the well-being of their children. The work cast doubt on legal and other procedures based on the premise of essentially rational conflict resolution thereby underestimating the primitive nature of the hostility between many couples who fail to act in the best interests of their children (Clulow and Vincent, 1987). Also arising from engagement with current social phenomena, clinical work in the IMS went alongside the provision of workshops for practitioners in a variety of settings in three diverse areas of the country. The aim was to compare experiences of work with clients when one or both partners in a marriage had become unemployed and to study the psychological impact of the loss of the opportunity to work. Attention was drawn to the reluctance of relevant professionals to involve themselves and reasons for this were investigated (Daniel, 1985; Mattinson, 1988).

The issues raised by *Marriage Matters,* particularly the need to promote interdisciplinary training and collaboration, were a continuing concern. When it became clear that no central initiative would materialise, a three-year training-cum-research programme was mounted involving fifty practitioners from front-line medical and non-medical services.[11] It focussed on the impact of marital stress on the five participating agencies and on the task-related anxieties impeding inter-professional collaboration (Woodhouse and Pengelly, forthcoming).

Alongside collaborative action research, there were successors to earlier endeavours in therapeutic practice and training. A study of a psychodynamic marital therapy echoed those of the past and highlighted the perceptions and subjective experience of the two therapists as much as those of the couple. But it extended previous work, paying further attention to the process of referral (from a general practitioner) and to the assessment of the outcome (Clulow, 1985). Similarly, factors relevant to brief marital work and the problem of assessing outcome were considered in another study (Clulow et al., 1986; Balfour et al., 1986). The couples in both instances were actively engaged in assessing the work, re-emphasising the original conception of the therapeutic encounter as a shared enterprise.

Extended experience of training groups for social work supervisors in an inner London local authority also drew on earlier IMS work when exploring the nature of the tension engendered by the supervisory role and of the anxiety commonly associated with it (Dearnley, 1985). And to long-established training programmes, two new courses were added: an internal one, the first of its kind in the U.K., leading to a Diploma in Marital Psychotherapy with an extra-mural Foundation Course linked to it.

Continuity was also evident in continuing collaboration with referring general practitioners; there was joint examination by a medical and an IMS practitioner of the way patients present marital stress to their family doctor (Cohen and Pugh, 1984). Meanwhile, therapeutic work prompted consideration of such contemporary issues as cross-cultural marriages (Cohen, 1982) and the effect of abortion on marriage (Mattinson, 1985). International work continues.[12]

Integrity and relevant uncertainty: present and future

As Clulow (1985) observed, the Greek word, 'therapy' is commonly assumed to mean *curing* or *healing*. Its first meaning is, however, *waiting on, serving, attending*. Marital therapy in the TIMS is a process of attending to couples and their unconsciously motivated interaction. It calls for informed listening, is reflective, essentially responsive and concerned with the mutual influence of couples and therapists. Just as it is clients who seek help, so in the unit's early years, training was offered in response to demand.

As we have seen, however, an interventionist, entrepreneurial mode had increasingly to be adopted alongside the responsive one with clients; the pursuit of financial viability had to go hand in hand with professional development. Pressure on limited resources increased; it was never possible to keep the contending claims of practice, training and research/publication in anything but uneasy equilibrium; the different work-patterns required in these three areas were often in conflict. But the overall outcome of managing these stresses has been creative. On the evidence, the culture developed by members of the working-group embodied an effective social system of defences against the anxieties inherent in the unit's therapeutic and other work and in its boundary position within and beyond the Tavistock (Menzies, 1970).

The nett effect of recent social and political trends has been to test the integrity of the TIMS and the coherence of its tripartite role. Progressively reduced financial support from central government and restrictions on local government services, leading to constraints on the Probation and Social Services, signify changes in political philosophy and social theory—and therefore attitudes towards the relationship between welfare and personal development.[13] Whether or not the changes in society are radical, or part of an oscillating process, only time will tell. But they and the contradictions previously noted are characteristic of an environment undergoing accelerating socio-technical change (Emery and Trist, 1972).

A good appreciation of the trends enabled time to be negotiated in which to become less dependent on direct public funding. In so doing the balance between technical development and financial necessity moved sharply towards the latter. The balance and reciprocal processes within the practice, training, research mix were seriously affected, giving rise to concern, not least as regards effects on the unit's core activity: service to clients, demands for which have escalated.

Changes in the field of care have inevitably affected the pattern of the unit's relationships within its professional network. Major points of reference for work with marriage and the family in non-medical public sector services have hitherto been probation and social work. Practitioners in these disciplines have, however, become increasingly concerned with techniques to deal with specific target groups. The trend has been away from casework with its emphasis on psychodynamic processes. Inevitably, the non-statutory marriage guidance movement has also been subject to the influence of social change and its repercussions. One of these has been fragmentation within the caring professions and a proliferation of many diverse forms of counselling and other types of help for personal problems.[14]

Training and consultation continue with members of all these professional groups; as would be expected, institutional change is uneven; some members continue to seek help from a psychodynamic approach to their practice.[15] Others, growing numbers of general practitioners, for example, are becoming more aware of the relational aspects of their primary task. The medical/social dichotomy, though still relevant to the TIMS, is less of an issue than it was, differences between psychodynamic approaches and those concerned with a 'technology of behaviour' (Barrett, 1979) have become more so. The areas of relevant uncertainty, to apply Trist's phrase, have widened considerably for the TIMS no less than for other practitioners in the field of care. Uncertainty generates anxiety.The evolution of the TIMS to date supports Menzies' proposition that 'the success and viability of a social institution are intimately connected with the techniques it uses to contain anxiety' (Menzies, 1970). Much will turn on the efficacy of the unit's social defence system in enabling members to maintain the integrity of the unit in the face of environmental changes different in kind and quality from those hitherto confronted.

Theoretical development

A note on theory

Turning now to concepts; their formulation results from the continuing need to make sense of the perplexities encountered by staff in therapeutic relationships with couples in marital difficulty, with each other in this context and, in training and project work, with colleagues in other settings. They are to be judged by their usefulness to practice. The assertion, attributed to Kurt Lewin, that 'there is nothing so practical as a good theory' captures the unit's attitudes as does Carl Jung's comment: 'Theories are not articles of faith; they are either instruments of knowledge and of therapy, or they are no good at all' (quoted by Mattinson and Sinclair, 1979).

What follows is atypical of TIMS literature, none of which is without case material, whether from therapy or other work, both as data and as illustration. The constraints of the present paper preclude such evidence and the illumination of interactive processes in relationships to be found in the cited text.

Conflict and anxiety within the person and in marriage

The partners bring to their relationship *all* their previous experience. This includes their internal, unconscious relationship systems. There is the person with a visible, acknowledged identity together with aspects of the personality which have been split off and repressed in the early stages of its development. These processes take place as a means of dealing with—that is, defending against—anxiety aroused because the needs inherent in these 'subselves' are experienced as incompatible and their expression impossible if reciprocal relationships with the environment are to be sustained. In this sense, the environment is comprised of objects upon which the child's development and indeed survival depends. First the relationship is with discreet aspects of the mother, later, mother as a whole person and then—the child having achieved a capacity to be related, as a human being, to two other human beings at the same time—mother and father and their relationship constitute the crucial environment; then the wider family and the world beyond it. The 'self' with these divisions is thus established in the earliest relationships at a time when a sense of well-being and of being well is bound up with bodily needs. As Winnicott (1956) puts it, '... in the child's dream, which is accompanied by bodily excitement, there is everything at stake'. Such patterning, the psychic purpose of which is to gain a sense of acceptance and security, has a major influence on later emotional development and, in particular, the capacity for relatedness, modes of attachment to others and for intimacy.

This view of the person mainly derives from the work of the 'object relations' school of psychoanalysis, though by no means exclusively so.[16] The schema indicates the conceptual framework found relevant in work with the several thousands of couples seen in the unit since it began and the many more considered with colleagues in other settings. An understanding of the legacies the partners bring to the relationship, and their influence on its characteristics and vulnerabilities, is based on it. Some facets may obtrude more than others in any given instance, but the part played by unconscious anxiety arising from conflictful relationships within the person and between the self and others is invariably central; the psychic strain and restrictive effects of maintaining defensive splits is all too obvious.

Emotional conflicts and growth

There can be no emotional growth without emotional conflict. Conflict does not invariably lead to growth but is an important ingredient of it. Change is inevitably feared when it threatens an identity evolved as a means of coping with unconscious anxiety. This is so even though the resulting partial experience of the self, perceptions of others and meanings ascribed to events give rise to unsatisfying or painful experience. Emotional growth, that is, maturation, involves the re-integration of and an altered relationship between those aspects of the self which have been split off, repressed, denied. It therefore means a modification of the image, including the sexual image the person has been impelled to assume and, through selective perception, has seen others as confirming—indeed has often coerced them into doing so. In some marriages, conflict between the partners has the quality of a 'fight to the death' reflecting the violence with which the internal image of the self is liable to be defended when it is felt to be threatened.

Marriage is a transference relationship 'par excellence'. The partners become a fundamental part of each other's environment; each is both subject and object and each is the object of the other's attachment. By its nature, the relationship is a primary one and the most direct heir to childhood experience in adult life. In it, emotive aspects of earlier actual and phantasy relationships are transferred by each onto the other; indeed their interplay ensures that unconsciously as well as consciously experienced aspects of the past, and the conflict and anxiety associated with them, are re-evoked—but in a new and present dimension. Thus, stress in marriage reflects conflict within the person, externalised and acted out in the partnership.

Shared defences, interaction and the potential for development

This process makes the internal dilemmas of each partner accessible through their interaction. As well as biological imperatives and the basic human need for attachment, such interaction reveals the developmental as well as the defensive potential of the dynamic relationship system in which both partners become deeply involved emotionally even if negatively. Such involvement is perhaps unremarkable in relationships of long-standing; together couples build up a psychobiological system, one which becomes enmeshed in and supported by a complex of social roles and responsibilities. However, therapeutic experience leads to the conclusion that the original choice of each by the other in any continuing relationship is unconsciously purposeful in that complementarity is a dominant feature; each recognises aspects of themselves, of which they are not consciously or willingly aware in the person of the other. Further, it shows that couples have deep-seated psychological preoccupations in common, notwithstanding differences in the way they may be articulated.

Developmental (and therefore therapeutic) potential lies in the fact that what is feared and rejected in the internal world, and is located in the person of the partner, is not lost but is 'lived with'. It is therefore available experientially and may be assimilated. Along with fear and rejection, there is evidence of a psychic need to reunite what Laing (1960) called the 'divided self'. Mainprice (1974) expressed it as follows:

> . . . there is a feeling that commitment and union can liberate. The hope that union can complete the incomplete and, at the same time, liberate the captive is quite general.

It appears in the thinking of people from different orientations and from different times. For instance, Teilhard de Chardin in 1959 had this to say, 'In every practical sphere, true union (that is to say synthesis) does not compound, it differentiates. Evidence of the fact that union differentiates is to be seen all around us'. And Heraclitus, in about 500 BC, stated the obverse: 'Men do not know how what is at variance agrees with itself. It is an attunement of opposite tensions, like that of the bow and the lyre'.

It will be clear that a basic role in marital interaction is ascribed to the defensive mechanism of projection and projective identification. Though not the only psychic defence, projection is a flexible one with the possibility that each partner may become more of a separate, autonomous person and less the receptacle of what the other rejects and denies. The process of withdrawing projections and of reintrojection is, however, precarious and fitful. Both partners are collusively involved and each may confirm the worst fears of the other, especially when an emotionally significant life event disturbs the equilibrium or change is attempted. Stress can become such that the containing function of the relationship (Jung, 1925) is threatened or overwhelmed. If help is sought then, it is the task of therapy to afford a 'breathing space' and a containing environment within which the implications of change for both partners may be tested. (Clulow, 1985; Lyons, 1973; Pincus, 1960; Guthrie and Mattinson, 1971; Woodhouse, 1975).

Constellations within dyadic systems are infinitely variable as are patterns of attachment, but couples can be conceived of as being on a scale. At one end are those where mutual defences support a shared unconscious purpose of the relationship which is anti-developmental—to avoid engagement with life. At the other are couples where the mutual value of defences lies in furthering the capacity to deal with internal conflict and external stress, supporting their containment and thus fostering growth (Morris, 1971). In terms of the defence of projection, developmental potential turns on *how much* of the personality is got rid of in this way; how *violent* is the mental act of projection; and the *rigidity* with which the defence is maintained.

Interactive processes in therapeutic relationships

A critical advance in marital work was to see that what the partners complained of in each other was an unwanted part of themselves (Sutherland, 1962). Caseworkers/therapists are also bound to become the object of their clients' projections, good and bad. With an emotionally significant relationship established, they too have transferred onto them feelings and attitudes arising from clients' internal needs which are not predominantly a reaction to the 'real' worker; and the worker's responses are bound to be affected.

At the beginning of the unit's life, the emphasis was mainly on enabling staff to manage the sometimes disturbing experiences to which sustained relationships with clients can give rise and on safeguarding them from inappropriate responses—countertransference in its original sense (Freud, 1910). Through supervision during training, and continuously in the work of the case conference, ways were found to help staff to become aware of these phenomena, to find an appropriate distance from clients and to distinguish between what in the work was a function of the client's and what of their own transference; to understand the detail of the former in any given case and accept professional responsibility for the latter. The use of the four-person therapeutic relationship was an added safeguard; being different people the countertransferences of the two caseworkers would also be different and, as previously noted, the interaction between the therapeutic pair and their subjective experience of each other was gradually recognized as an added source of information about the dilemmas in their clients' relationship (Pincus, 1960). To give a simple example: it was (and is) a commonplace in four-person work for one of the therapeutic pair to feel that their colleague is colluding with one or other client to the detriment of the work. They may be. But how these differences are articulated and the difficulty of their resolution is frequently found to be an unconscious reaction to the clients at this point in the work, and for the workers' behaviour to have important similarities with the couple's defence against anxiety in confronting specific differences. The process and its meaning may only become clear when the case is presented at conference—this even though regular time for discussion between those sharing the work is a formal part of the therapeutic procedure.

Recognition that such reactions were not solely a product of the personal or technical deficiencies of workers was contemporary with what Mattinson (1975) saw as the widening and enriching of the concept of countertransference by those 'who perceived the countertransference as a function of the transference of the client. The reaction of the worker to the clients' transference need not be condemned, but could be noted and used for increasing the understanding of the clients' behaviour.'

Following Searles (1959), she summarised the IMS position on countertransference in therapeutic interaction as:

an innate and inevitable ingredient

which is sometimes a conscious reaction to the observed behaviour of the client, or which is sometimes an unconscious reaction to the felt and not consciously understood behaviour of the client

and which can be used for increasing understanding of the client [in addition] . . .

the resolution by the worker of the countertransference [is] one of the main ingredients of casework which enables the client to resolve and relinquish the transference

It is not that classical countertransference—that is, workers' transference—is disregarded as a factor militating against effective therapy. It is the change of emphasis that is important, one which points to the need for workers to be free to engage with clients in a human interaction within a structured, containing therapeutic environment. They have to discover what, for each of them, is the appropriate closeness to and distance from their clients in the knowledge that 'you can exert no influence if you are not susceptible to influence' (Jung, 1931); that emotional involvement is the vehicle for change; that without it one is denied the opportunity to learn about critical aspects of clients' unconscious intra- and interpersonal conflicts which, being so, cannot be expressed in words.

Interactive processes in training: the 'reflection' process

In the light of the foregoing, it is noteworthy that the TIMS was slow to recognise the full implications for training and trainers of what had come to be taken for granted in the unit's practice: explicit attempts to make use of the workers' unrecognised responses to clients' unconscious defences against anxiety. This experience had indeed been taken into training aimed at helping practitioners develop understanding and skill in work with marital and related family stress relevant to their own setting and field of work. But so far as trainers were concerned, the emphasis had remained on helping them extend *their own* casework in the firm belief that what the teacher can offer trainees is bounded by their own practice experience. Not that all practitioners can be good teachers, but that the teaching of those whose practice is limited will be similarly so and unresourceful.

In retrospect it can be seen that the prevailing climate was a product of the unit's preoccupation with the preservation and development of its own specialty and of the conservatism that is an inherent ingredient of change (Marris, 1974). It also points to the gradualness with which wider applications were made of the 'open systems' concept, which was integral to the view of the person and of marital and family relationships that had evolved.

An example of the creative potential of long-term interaction with those in the field and of a culture developed out of the sometimes fraught experience of mutual influence was referred to earlier: work with a group of field-work supervisors of social work students and their university colleagues. The supervisors insisted that attention be paid to their supervisory problems as well as their own practice. Shared work on these issues enabled material to be assembled supporting the thesis, first put forward by Searles (1955) arising from his supervision of analytic work with psychiatric patients, to the effect that processes at work currently in the relationship between client and worker are often reflected in the relationship between worker and supervisor. Searles used the term 'reflection process' to describe this mirroring phenomena, one adopted in the report and discussion of the work with supervisors (Mattinson, 1975).

Simple of expression, the application of the concept can be more difficult in practice, the processes often being subtle in their manifestation. It involves appreciation of variables already indicated, namely: of the degree of involvement with the client that trainee workers or staff members are able to allow themselves; of the strength and flexibility of workers' psychological boundaries (a personal dimension); of the capacity of the setting to facilitate and contain the work and its associated anxiety (an institutional dimension); of the distinction between conscious and unconscious countertransference (for example, negative countertransference may be a response to the client's projections, but it may also be a conscious reaction to objectively unpleasant or abhorrent aspects of their behaviour which are not understood); and, not so far mentioned, of the extent to which the worker's responses are out of character and defensive, this being an indication of the degree of disturbance encountered.

This recapitulation lays emphasis on the worker. The full range of the reflection process is evidenced when a third party (the supervisor in this instance) also reacts unconsciously. That is to say, when there is acting out in response to the trainee and his material which, while it may convey his consciously felt anxiety, is false and leads to an impasse between them. It was a supervisor's bewildered discomfort at her persistent and uncharacteristically 'waspish' treatment of an apparently impenetrable student, whose defensive lack of involvement in the supervision was seen to be similar to that of a mother with her delinquent son, that focussed attention on the process. It is one through which unconscious defences against anxiety within one relationship system (the client's) can be carried over, via the 'bridging' worker, into another adjacent one. When the meaning of this kind of interaction is unravelled, understanding of the client's defence is advanced and the trainee's work can change.

*Interaction within institutions:
clients, workers and their organisations*

As just noted, the institutional dimension is an important variable bearing on the worker's response to clients and their relationships. Training work had shown that marital problems were intimidating for subjective as much as technical reasons. Working with a focus on a couple's interaction could threaten the psychological distance social workers were generally enabled to maintain between themselves and clients when addressing the particular difficulties their agencies were established to treat—delinquency, mental illness, child neglect, for example. Marriage, however, was often 'too near home for comfort'. For the majority, their specialized institutional setting provided little or no support in managing this boundary and the anxiety engendered by work with the intimate relationship of marriage (E. Balint, 1959; Woodhouse, 1967a).

By the mid-1970s organisational boundaries in the personal social services had changed; many of the specialized services had been amalgamated;[17] social workers, like their agencies, now had multiple roles and tasks. These changes and a better grasp of the functioning of open systems required a fresh assessment. Hence the importance, in the present context, of the local authority Social Services department project referred to earlier and of the relevance of the direct experience of the IMS staff when practising alongside social work colleagues as basic grade workers in the department.

The evidence suggested that a large proportion of the department's time and resources was devoted to a core group of married clients with severe relationship problems, one it was ill adapted to treat. These clients evoked ambivalent responses from social workers who wished to help but feared being overwhelmed. Worker-client interaction was liable to reinforce the pattern of ambivalent attachments and the defences of denial and splitting dominating the clients' lives. The culture and mode of functioning of the organisation, itself under pressure from proliferating demand and increasingly restricted resources, abetted practitioners in avoiding or defending against the anxiety inherent in providing the kind of reliable, sustained though time-limited help appropriate to these deprived and demanding clients. Indeed, the institutional framework, in association with the clients, in itself stimulated anxiety. It diminished the ability to address their practical and emotional problems as interdependent and to do marital work.

While Bowlby's theory of attachment and loss (Bowlby, 1969, 1973, 1980) proved the most relevant to an understanding of the relatively small but highly influential core group of clients and their troubled relationships, Menzies' (1970) study of social systems as a defence against anxiety enabled sense to be made of the interplay between social workers and their overburdened organisation. She emphasises that defences can only be operated by individuals; a social system as such cannot operate a defence, but 'when the need of the member is to defend against what is felt to be intolerable anxiety the organisation will be used for that purpose'.

Concerning the problem of engendering change in local authority Social Services, the setting in which the majority of social workers operate, Mattinson and Sinclair (1979) point out that,

> If the workers are continually subjected to the splitting mechanisms of [these] clients, they too may become predisposed to this mode of behaviour, and as the individual worker can reflect his client's defence, so too may some of the organizational practices which the worker is expected to perform. The problem is that whereas the individual worker may eventually use his reflection constructively in understanding the client's emotional problem, it is much more difficult for the organisation as a whole to do this once a particular practice has become institutionalized. Unfortunately, just as the resistance to change is believed to be greatest in clients exercising the most primitive psychic defences (and splitting is a very primitive defence), so group resistance to social change may be greatest in social systems also dominated by this mode.

It may be noted that institutional resistance to change helps to explain the constraints on the outcome of training noted earlier. Trainees are potential 'change agents'. Their attempts to introduce new perspectives on practice may be met by ambivalence if at variance with established social defences. Reviewing a training course and their subsequent working experience, a group of well-established probation officers reported feeling 'like Christians in the catacombs' back in their agency.

Interaction between institutions: interprofessional collaboration

The Social Services Department project graphically confirmed what had been learned from clinical work in the IMS and from training: that there is a strong tendency for the internal problems of individuals, couples and families to be externalized and to be mirrored by the relationship between practitioners to the detriment of collaboration. More recently other therapists have commented on the same processes (e.g. Reder, 1983; Will, 1983). Britton (1981) coined the phrase 'complementary acting out' to describe their manifestations at the level of the service network.

However, it is clear that practitioners are not passive recipients of clients' projections. Not only do they have personal susceptibilities to anxiety and idiosyncratic ways of defending against it which they take into the work, they operate defences which are embedded in their agency's culture and expressed in its rules, organisational procedures and ways of interpreting policy.

> An important aspect of such socially structured defence mechanisms is an attempt by individuals to externalize and give substance in objective reality to their characteristic psychic defence mechanisms. A social defence system develops over time as a result of collusive interaction and agreement, often unconscious, between members of the organisation as to what form it shall take. The socially structured mechanisms then tend to become an aspect of external reality with which old and new members must come to terms. [Menzies, 1960]

The common need for defences against anxiety is an important factor in the cohesion of associations (Jacques, 1955); those whose psychological needs are sufficiently met by the prevailing social defence mechanisms will support and seek to preserve them. The alternative is to leave. Even a worker with mature ways of coping with personal anxiety will find it hard to resist a well-developed professional or agency defence, particularly if, as is often the case, the nature of the work arouses strong and primitive anxieties (Hornby, 1983).

The programme referred to earlier (Woodhouse and Pengelly, forthcoming) involved the study of work with more than a hundred cases that preoccupied experienced workers (including doctors in the Family Practitioner Service) in one locality. It lasted three years and was mainly conducted in mixed-discipline workshops. The majority of the worrying cases brought into the programme raised just such strong and primitive anxieties.

Anxieties of this kind and quality can threaten a practitioner's sense of professional adequacy and personal autonomy. The defences discussed by Hornby (1983) were variously enacted by participating practitioners in their work and in the programme: denial to avoid experiencing envy of other workers' opportunities and skills; displacement of hostility; splitting off and projecting feelings of inadequacy; and, especially in the few cases worked jointly, projective identification which could ensure that skill and competence was vested in one practitioner, uselessness and helplessness in another. The defensive use of boundaries—around the worker/client or doctor/patient relationship, or around agencies—was also prominent. The testing of mutual perceptions through working relationships was generally avoided, and the tendency of practitioners to isolate themselves from one another was evidenced in case discussion and reports which showed workers behaving as if colleagues in other agencies, relevant to the work, did not exist, or were unapproachable.

Collaboration involves the exploration of differences and the revelation of uncertainty. Such experience in itself can generate depressive and persecutory anxiety which takes time to modify. This was achieved to some extent and in varying degrees among participants in the containing and enabling environment the programme aimed to provide. It represented a 'temporary institution', analogues of which are difficult to establish in local service networks, a fact recognised in *Marriage Matters* by the recommendation that local multi-disciplinary training and development groups be established (Home Office, 1979).

All the processes described impede collaboration, but there is a further and more entrenched one. The socially structured defence mechanisms operating in agencies and professional groups, while they have features in common, are distinctive. They stem from the unconscious as well as the conscious anxiety inherent in the tasks practitioners are employed to perform. In the programme here referred to, for example, they related to doctors' work with the sick and dying; to that of health visitors (community nurses) with mothers and babies and conflictful mother/child relationships; to marriage counsellors and their work with stress in intimate heterosexual relationships; to probation officers with delinquents and tensions between conformity and individual liberty; and to social workers with the disturbed and rejected and with parents who fail to care adequately for their children.

However, such tasks afford practitioners their professional identity as well as the sentient group with which they identify and on which they depend for emotional support (Miller and Rice, 1967). Defences against anxiety associated with the task command deep emotional loyalty. They characterise organisations, but their unconscious origins and function are seldom manifest in situations where they are accessible to the kind of work-related scrutiny that can facilitate modification and the mastery of anxiety. Socially organized defences against anxiety must therefore be counted among the reasons why institutions and their behaviour are so resistant to change.

When workers share responsibility for clients or patients or engage in joint work, incompatibilities between agency defences tend to emerge. These are accentuated when the clients involved employ primitive projective defences, when their difficulties give rise to high levels of objective anxiety and, at the same time, stimulate powerful unconscious phantasies. The higher the level of anxiety, the greater the reliance on institutionalized defences is likely to be and the more emotionally hazardous it becomes for practitioners to enter into each other's working-world for fear of losing hold of their own. Thus, in situations where collaboration is at a premium, as when children are 'at risk', it is often most difficult to achieve.

Other factors also influence inter-professional and inter-agency relationships. Some emanate from the personal characteristics of individuals; some are structural; others have to do with values, status and professional and wider politics. Dire consequences can follow failure in inter-professional and inter-agency collaboration. When they do, and public concern leads to official enquiry, the refinement of practice guidelines and improved administrative and legal procedures are mainly looked to for remedy. Valuable and necessary as these are in themselves, such rational prescriptions commonly fail to embody recognition of what Will and Baird (1984) have called 'real inter-professional vulnerabilities'. Gross failures in collaboration between practitioners and agencies are invariably multi-faceted. Unless the inevitability of intense unconscious anxiety and conflict is acknowledged and their corollaries in institutionalized as well as personal defences against them are accepted rather than denied or condemned, improved working relationships, especially under stressful conditions, are likely to remain elusive.

In conclusion

The debt the TIMS owes to the work of others in and beyond the Tavistock will have been obvious. It is considerable to colleagues in community services, but greatest to its clients. Marital therapy has proved a powerful stimulus. The meaning and purpose of stress and conflict in the relationship between couples point towards an integrated approach to understanding impediments to creative interaction within and between the discreet but interdependent open systems that constitute the caring services.

NOTES

1. Enid Eichholz, later Enid Balint.
2. Report on Procedure in Matrimonial Causes, 1947: London, H.M.S.O.—the 'Denning Report'; Report of the Departmental Committee on Grants for the Development of Marriage Guidance, 1948: London, H.M.S.O.—the 'Harris Report'.
3. Administrative separation of Clinic and Institute was achieved in 1947 in preparation for the Clinic's entry into the National Health Service. Operationally, the two bodies remained very close at that time; from the point of view of the experimental FWA group, the distinction was of little significance: the working relationship was with 'the Tavistock'.
4. Michael Balint from the Tavistock Clinic (he and Enid Eichholz were married in 1953); Isabel Menzies, E. L. Trist and A. T. M. Wilson from TIHR. When the Balints later turned to work with general practitioners, J. D. Sutherland (who had been associated with the F.D.B. experiment from the outset) and A. G. Thompson took over the role of analytically trained psychiatric consultants. After an interval Enid Balint resumed and still continues her association with the unit as consultant and supervisor.
5. Lily Pincus succeeded Enid Balint in 1953 and chaired the staff group till 1963.
6. Dr Ronald Hargreaves, who became the first head of the Mental Health Section of the World Health Organisation.
7. In the main, those attending are professionals and their spouses, one or both of whose work affects the lives of many other people. Those in the caring professions are prominent among clients.
8. The marital unit in the Tavistock Clinic under the direction of H. V. Dicks employed three-person therapy as being appropriate to a medical setting and his department's resources. The work led to the concept of 'the shared internal object', important in the diagnosis and treatment of marital tensions (Teruel, 1966; Dicks, 1967).
9. The committee made wide-ranging proposals to achieve 'a community-based and family oriented service which will be available to all' (Seebohm, 1968). The Local Authority Personal Social Services Act, 1970, followed. The analysis underlying recommendations for the large, ubiquitous Social Services Departments that came into being owed little to a psychodynamic appreciation of the problems addressed. For a critique and discussion of some implications of work with marital problems in such a setting, see Mattinson and Sinclair (1979).

10. The IMS had at last been able to move towards achieving the size and balance seen to be necessary twenty years earlier. At the beginning of the 1960s, the permanent staff had been equivalent to 6½ full-time members, mostly women. By 1979, the figure was just over 10, the sexes almost equally represented.

11. Although no central initiative followed the publication of *Marriage Matters,* the Home Office, which, with the Department of Health and Social Security, established the working party that produced it, made a grant towards the cost of the IMS programme.

12. An annual international summer school began in 1983. Links are maintained with colleagues in Europe and beyond. The chairmanship of the Commission on Marriage and Inter-personal Relations of the International Union of Family Organisations passed to the IMS in 1986.

13. The influence of these changes is, of course, widespread. Health and education as well as welfare services have been greatly affected. As Sutherland (1980) points out, the three comprise an interdependent triad which, when administratively treated as such, as in the United States, reflects political recognition that development is the best form of welfare.

14. Moves were made in the mid-1970s to regulate psychotherapy through registration. Progress was slow, but following the publication of the consultative document *Marriage Matters* (Home Office, 1979) the British Association of Counselling provided fresh impetus and a Standing Conference for Psychotherapy was established. The Conference is endeavouring to establish a constitution that will accommodate the wide diversity now represented in the membership.

15. One outcome of their continuing influence has been the establishment of the Group for the Advancement of Psychodynamics and Psychotherapy in Social Work (GAPS) and, since 1983, the publication of its *Journal of Social Work Practice.*

16. Some authors whose work was referred to in the unit's original theoretical account of personality development (Pincus, 1960) elaborated their formulations subsequently; other contributions to the literature also influence current practice. (See, for example, Balint, 1968; Bowlby, 1969, 1973, 1980; Fairbairn, 1954; Fordham, 1957; Freud, 1893–95, 1926; Guntrip, 1968; Jung, 1940, 1953; Klein, 1932, 1957; Klein and Riviere, 1939; Sutherland, 1958, 1983; Winnicott, 1956, 1971, 1975).

17. When, in 1970, the local authority personal social services were reorganized in England and Wales the Probation Service retained its autonomy; in Scotland it became an integral part of the social services system.

REFERENCES

Balfour, F., Clulow, C., & Dearnley, B. (1986). The outcome of a maritally focussed psychotherapy offered as a possible model for marital psychotherapy outcome studies. *British Journal of Psychotherapy, 3*: 133–143.

Balint, E. (1959). Training postgraduate students in social casework. *British Journal of Medical Psychology, 32*: 193–199.

Balint, M. (1954). Method and technique in the teaching of medical psychology, II. Training general practitioners in psychotherapy. *British Journal of Medical Psychology, 27*: 37–41.

────── . (1964). *The Doctor, His Patient and the Illness* (second edition). London: Pitman Medical.

────── . (1968). *The Basic Fault: Therapeutic Aspects of Regression*. London: Tavistock Publications.

Bannister, K., Lyons, A., Pincus, L., Robb, J., Shooter, A., & Stephens, J. (1955). *Social Casework in Marital Problems*. London: Tavistock Publications.

Bannister, K., & Pincus, L. (1965). *Shared Phantasy in Marital Problems: Therapy in a Four-Person Relationship*. London: Institute of Marital Studies.

———. (1966). Seminars on marital interaction for social workers in Israel. *Social Work, 23*: 3–11.
Barrett, W. (1979). *The Illusion of Technique*. London: William Kimber.
Berger, P. L., & Kellner, H. (1964). Marriage and the construction of reality. *Diogenes*, pp. 1–23.
Bernard, J. (1973). *The Future of Marriage*. New York: Yale University Press.
Bion, W. R. (1961). *Experience in Groups*. London: Tavistock Publications.
Bott, E. (1957). *Family and Social Network*. London: Tavistock Publications.
Bowlby, J. (1949). The Study and Reduction of Group Tensions in the Family. *Human Relations, 2*: 123–128
———. (1969). *Attachment and Loss. Volume I: Attachment*. London: The Hogarth Press and The Institute of Psycho-Analysis.
———. (1973). *Attachment and Loss. Volume II: Separation, Anxiety and Anger*. London: The Hogarth Press and The Institute of Psycho-Analysis.
———. (1980). *Attachment and Loss. Volume III: Loss, Sadness and Depression*. London: The Hogarth Press and The Institute of Psycho-Analysis.
Britton, R. (1981). Re-enactment as an unwitting professional response to family dynamics. In S. Box, B. Copley, J. Magagna, & E. Moustaki (eds.), *Psychotherapy with Families*. London: Routledge and Kegan Paul.
Burgoyne, J., & Clark, D. (1984). *Making a Go of It*. London: Routledge and Kegan Paul.
Burgoyne, J., Ormrod, R., & Richards, M. (1987). *Divorce Matters*. Harmondsworth, Middlesex: Penguin.
Butler-Sloss, E. (1988). Report of the Inquiry into Child Abuse in Cleveland, 1987. London: H.M.S.O.
Clulow, C. F. (1982). *To Have and to Hold: Marriage, the First Baby and Preparing Couples for Parenthood*. Aberdeen: Aberdeen University Press.
———. (1985). *Marital Therapy: An Inside View*. Aberdeen: Aberdeen University Press.
Clulow, C. F., Dearnley, B., & Balfour, F. (1986). Shared phantasy and therapeutic structure in a brief marital psychotherapy. *British Journal of Psychotherapy, 3*: 124–132.

Clulow, C. F., & Mattinson, J. (1989). *Marriage Inside Out. Understanding Problems of Intimacy.* Harmondsworth, Middlesex: Penguin.

Clulow, C. F., & Vincent, C. (1987). *In the Child's Best Interests.* London: Tavistock, Sweet and Maxwell.

Cmnd. 9678. (1956). *Royal Commission on Marriage and Divorce.* H.M.S.O.

Cohen, N. (1982). Same or different? A problem of identity in cross cultural marriages. *Journal of Family Therapy, 4*: 177–199.

Cohen, N., & Pugh, G. (1984). The presentation of marital problems in general practice. *The Practitioner, 228*: 651–656.

Colman, W. (1989). *On Call. The Work of a Telephone Helpline for Child Abuse.* Aberdeen: Aberdeen University Press.

Daniel, D. (1985). Love and work: Complementary aspects of personal identity. *International Journal of Social Economics, 12* (2): 48–55.

Dearnley, B. (1985). A plain man's guide to supervision—or new clothes for the Emperor? *Journal of Social Work Practice, 2*: 52–65.

Dicks, H. V. (1967). *Marital Tensions.* London: Routledge and Kegan Paul.

——— . (1970). *Fifty Years of the Tavistock Clinic.* London: Routledge and Kegan Paul.

Emery, F. E., & Trist, E. L. (1972). *Towards a Social Ecology. Contextual Appreciation of the Future in the Present.* London: Plenum Publishing Company.

Fairbairn, W. R. (1954). *An Object Relations Theory of the Personality.* New York: Basic Books.

Fordham, M. (1957). *New Developments in Analytical Psychology.* London: Routledge and Kegan Paul.

Freud, S. (1895d [1893–95]). With Breuer, J. *Studies on Hysteria. Standard Edition, 2.* London: The Hogarth Press and The Institute of Psycho-Analysis.

——— . (1910d). The future prospects of psycho-analytic therapy. *Standard Edition, 11.* London: The Hogarth Press and The Institute of Psycho-Analysis.

——— . (1926d [1925]). *Inhibitions, Symptoms and Anxiety. Standard Edition, 20.* London: The Hogarth Press and The Institute of Psycho-Analysis.

Gray, S. G. (1970). The Tavistock Institute of Human Relations. In

H. V. Dicks, *Fifty Years of the Tavistock Clinic*. London: Routledge and Kegan Paul.

Guntrip, H. S. (1968). *Schizoid Phenomena, Object Relations and the Self*. New York: International Universities Press.

Guthrie, L., & Mattinson, J. (1971). *Brief Casework with a Marital Problem*. London: Institute of Marital Studies.

Herbert, W. L., & Jarvis, F. V. (1959). *A Modern Approach to Marriage Counselling*. London: Methuen.

Home Office (1979). *Marriage Matters*. London: Her Majesty's Stationery Office.

Hornby, S. (1983). Collaboration in social work: A major practice issue. *The Journal of Social Work Practice, 1*: 35–55.

Institute of Marital Studies (1962). *The Marital Relationship as a Focus for Casework*. London: Institute of Marital Studies.

Jaques, E. (1955). Social systems as a defence against persecutory and depressive anxiety. In M. Klein, P. Heimann, & R. E. Money-Kyrle (eds.), *New Directions in Psychoanalysis*. London: Tavistock Publications.

Jung, C. (1925). Marriage as a psychological relationship in the development of personality. *Collected Works, Volume 17*. London: Routledge and Kegan Paul, 1954.

―――― . (1931). Problems of modern psychotherapy. *Collected Works, Volume 16*. London: Routledge and Kegan Paul, 1954.

―――― . (1940). The psychology of the child archetype. *Collected Works, Volume 9*. London: Routledge and Kegan Paul, 1954.

―――― . (1953). The development of personality. *Collected Works, Volume 17*. London: Routledge and Kegan Paul, 1954.

Kinsey, A. C., Pomeroy, W. B., & Martin, C. E. (1948). *Sexual Behaviour in the Human Male*. Philadelphia, PA: Saunders.

Kinsey, A. C., Pomeroy, W. B., Martin, C. E., & Gebhard, P. H. (1953). *Sexual Behavior in the Human Female*. Philadelphia, PA: Saunders.

Klein, M. (1932). *The Psycho-Analysis of Children*. London: The Hogarth Press.

―――― . (1957). *Envy and Gratitude: A Study of Unconcious Sources*. London: Tavistock Publications.

Klein, M., & Riviere, J. (1939). *Love, Hate and Reparation*. London: The Hogarth Press.

Laing, R. D. (1960). *The Divided Self*. London: Tavistock Publications.

Lasch, C. (1977) *Haven in a Heartless World*. New York: Basic Books.

Lewis, J. M., Beavers, W. R., Gossett, J. T., & Phillips, V. A. (1976). *No Single Thread: Psychological Health in Family Systems*. New York: Brunner/Mazel.

Lyons, A. (1973). Therapeutic intervention in relation to the institution of marriage. In Robert Gosling (ed.), *Support, Innovation and Autonomy* (pp. 173–186). London: Tavistock Publications.

Mace, D. (1948). *Marriage Crisis*. London: Delisle.

Mainprice, J. (1974). *Marital Interaction and Some Illnesses in Children*. London: Institute of Marital Studies.

Marris, P. (1974). *Loss and Change*. Routledge and Kegan Paul.

Masters, W. H., & Johnson, V. E. (1966). *Human Sexual Response*. Boston, MA: Little, Brown.

——— . *Human Sexual Inadequacy*. Boston, MA: Little, Brown.

Mattinson, J. (1970). *Marriage and Mental Handicap*. London: Duckworth; paperback. London: Institute of Marital Studies, 1975.

——— . (1975). *The Reflection Process in Casework Supervision*. London: Institute of Marital Studies.

——— . (1981). The deadly equal triangle. In *Change and Renewal in Psychodynamic Social Work: British and American Developments in Practice and Education for Services to Families and Children*. Massachusetts and London: Smith College School of Social Work and Group for the Advancement of Psychotherapy in Social Work.

——— . (1985). The effects of abortion on marriage. In CIBA Foundation Symposium 115, *Abortion: Medical Progress and Social Implications* (pp. 165–172). London: Pitman.

——— . (1988). *Work, Love and Marriage: The Impact of Unemployment*. London: Duckworth.

Mattinson, J., & Sinclair, I. (1979). *Mate and Stalemate: Working with Marital Problems in a Social Services Department*. Oxford: Blackwell; paperback: London, Institute of Marital Studies, 1981.

Menzies, I. E. P. (1949). Factors affecting family breakdown in urban communities. *Human Relations, 2*: 363–373.

——— . (1970). *The Functioning of Social Systems as a Defence against Anxiety*. London: Tavistock Institute of Human Relations.

Miller, E. J., & Rice, A. K. (1967). *Systems of Organisation*. London: Tavistock Publications.

Mount, F. (1983). *The Subversive Family*. London: Allen and Unwin.

Morgan, D. H. J. (1985). *The Family, Politics and Social Theory*. London: Routledge and Kegan Paul.

Morris, B. (1971). An educational perspective on mental health. In J. D. Sutherland (ed.), *Towards Community Mental Health* (pp. 31–46). London: Tavistock Publications.

Neumann, J. von, & Morgenstern, O. (1947). *Theory of Games and Economic Behaviour*. Princeton, NJ: Princeton University Press.

Pincus, L. (ed.) (1960). *Marriage: Studies in Emotional Conflict and Growth*. London: Methuen; paperback. London: Institute of Marital Studies, 1973.

Reder, P. (1983). Disorganised families and the helping professions: 'who's in charge of what?' *Journal of Family Therapy*, 1: 23–36.

Rice, A. K. (1965). *Learning for Leadership. Interpersonal and Intergroup Relations*. London: Tavistock Publications.

Searles, H. F. (1955). The informational value of the supervisor's emotional experience. In *Collected Papers on Schizophrenia and Related Subjects*. London: The Hogarth Press and the Institute of Psycho-Analysis, 1965.

―――― . (1959). Oedipal love in the countertransference. In *Collected Papers on Schizophrenia and Related Subjects*. London: The Hogarth Press and the Institute of Psycho-Analysis.

Seebohm, F. (1968). *Report of the Committee on Local Authority and Allied Personal Social Services*. London: Her Majesty's Stationery Office, Cmnd. 3703.

Shannon, C. E., & Weaver, W. (1949). *The Mathematical Theory of Communication*. Urbana, IL: University of Illinois Press.

Skynner, R., & Cleese, J. *Families & How to Survive Them*. London: Methuen.

Sutherland, J. D. (1955). Introduction. In K. Bannister, A. Lyons, L. Pincus, J. Robb, A. Shooter, & J. Stephens, *Social Casework in Marital Problems*. London: Tavistock Publications.

―――― . (1956). Psychotherapy and social casework, I. In E. M. Goldberg, E. E. Irvine, A. B. Lloyd Davies, & K. F. McDougal, *The Boundaries of Casework*. London: Association of Psychiatric Social Workers.

―――― . (ed.) (1958). *Psycho-Analysis and Contemporary Thought*. International Psycho-Analytical Library, No. 53. London: The Hogarth Press and The Institute of Psycho-Analysis.

———. (1962). Introduction. In *The Marital Relationship as a Focus for Casework*. London: Institute of Marital Studies.

———. (1963). Object relations theory and the conceptual model of psycho-analysis. *British Journal of Medical Psychology, 36*: 109–120.

———. (1967). The place of psychotherapy in community mental health. The Margaret Allan Lecture. *Contact, 19*: 1–18.

———. (1968). The consultant psychotherapist in the National Health Service; his role and training. *The British Journal of Psychiatry, 114*: 509–515.

———. (1971). Introduction. In J. D. Sutherland (ed.), *Towards Community Mental Health*. London: Tavistock Publications.

———. (1980). *The Psychodynamic Image of Man: A Philosophy for the Caring Professions*. Aberdeen: Aberdeen University Press.

———. (1983). The self and object relations. A challenge to psychoanalysis. *Bulletin of the Menninger Foundation, 47*: 525–541.

TIMS. (1988). *Parting Company: The Impact of Separation*. TIMS/Rolf Harris video.

TIMS. (1988). *Unemployment and Marriage*. TIMS/Rolf Harris video.

Teruel, G. (1966). Considerations for a diagnosis in marital psychotherapy. *British Journal of Medical Psychology, 39*: 231–236.

Trist, E. L., & Sofer, C. (1959). *Explorations in Group Relations*. Leicester: Leicester University Press.

Vaillant, G. (1977). *Adaptation to Life*. Boston, MA: Little, Brown.

Weeks, J. (1981). *Sex, Politics and Society*. London: Longmans.

Wiener, N. (1948). *Cybernetics*. New York: John Wiley.

Will, D. (1983). Some techniques for working with resistant families of adolescents. *Journal of Adolescence, 6*: 13–26.

Will, D., & Baird, D. (1984). An integrated approach to dysfunction in inter-professional systems. *Journal of Family Therapy, 6*: 275–290.

Wilson, A. T. M. (1947a). The development of a scientific basis in family casework. *Social Work, 4*: 62–69.

———. (1947b). Some implications of medical practice and social casework for action research. *Journal of Social Issues, 3* (2): 11–28.

———. (1949). Some reflections and suggestions on the prevention and treatment of marital problems. *Human Relations, 2*: 233–251.

———. (1951). A note on some current problems of the social services. *Social Work, 8*: 504–514.

Wilson, A. T. M., Menzies, I., & Eichholz, E. (1949). Report of the Marriage Welfare Sub-committee of the Family Welfare Association. *Social Work, 6*: 258–262.

Winnicott, D. W. (1956). Paediatrics and childhood neurosis. In *Through Paediatrics to Psycho-analysis*. London: The Hogarth Press and the Institute of Psycho-Analysis, 1975.

———. (1971). *Playing and Reality*. London: Tavistock Publications.

Woodhouse, D. (1967a). Short residential courses for post-graduate social workers. In R. H. Gosling, D. H. Miller, D. Woodhouse, & P. M. Turquet, *The Use of Small Groups in Training* (pp. 76–97). London: Tavistock Institute of Medical Psychology and Condicote Press.

———. (1967b). The marital relationship. In *Human Growth and Behaviour as a Subject of Study for Social Workers* (pp. 21–22). London: Council for Training in Social Work.

———. (1969). Marital problems: a strategy for service and research. In J. Marshall (ed.), *The Future of Christian Marriage* (pp. 110–112). London: Chapman.

———. (1970). *Interactie in het huwelijk*. Utrecht: Spectrum.

———. (1975). Personal development and marital interaction. *Marriage Guidance, 15*: 359–368.

Woodhouse, D. L., & Pengelly, P. J. C. (forthcoming). *Anxiety and the Dynamics of Collaboration*.

Young, M., & Willmott, P. (1957). *Family and Kinship in East London*. London: Routledge and Kegan Paul.

Younghusband, E. L. (1947). *Report on the Employment and Training of Social Workers*. Carnegie United Kingdom Trust.